Knowledge Management

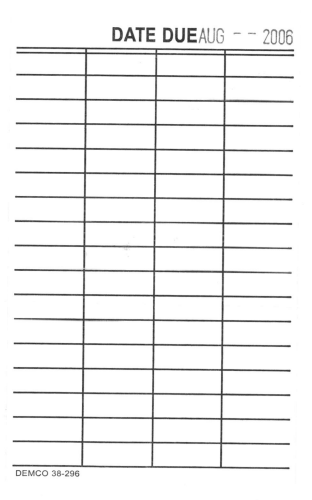

CHANDOS
INFORMATION PROFESSIONAL SERIES

Series Editor: Ruth Rikowski
(email: rikowski@tiscali.co.uk)

Chandos' new series of books are aimed at the busy information professional. They have been specially commissioned to provide the reader with an authoritative view of current thinking. They are designed to provide easy-to-read and (most importantly) practical coverage of topics that are of interest to librarians and other information professionals. If you would like a full listing of current and forthcoming titles, please visit our web site **www.library-chandospublishing.com** or contact Hannah Grace-Williams on email info@chandospublishing.com or telephone number +44 (0) 1865 884447.

New authors: we are always pleased to receive ideas for new titles; if you would like to write a book for Chandos, please contact Dr Glyn Jones on email gjones@chandospublishing.com or telephone number +44 (0) 1865 884447.

Bulk orders: some organisations buy a number of copies of our books. If you are interested in doing this, we would be pleased to discuss a discount. Please contact Hannah Grace-Williams on email info@chandospublishing.com or telephone number +44 (0) 1865 884447.

Knowledge Management

Cultivating knowledge professionals

SULIMAN AL-HAWAMDEH

Chandos Publishing

Oxford · England · New Hampshire · USA

Chandos Publishing (Oxford) Limited
Chandos House
5 & 6 Steadys Lane
Stanton Harcourt
Oxford OX29 5RL
UK
Tel: +44 (0) 1865 884447 Fax: +44 (0) 1865 884448
Email: info@chandospublishing.com
www.library-chandospublishing.com

Chandos Publishing USA
3 Front Street, Suite 331
PO Box 338
Rollinsford, NH 03869
USA
Tel: 603 749 9171 Fax: 603 749 6155
Email: BizBks@aol.com

First published in Great Britain in 2003

ISBN:
1 84334 037 2 (paperback)
1 84334 038 0 (hardback)

© S. Al-Hawamdeh, 2003

Typeset by Concerto, Leighton Buzzard, Bedfordshire, UK (01525 378757)
Printed in the UK and USA

Contents

Preface

Until recently, information specialists played the role of gatekeeper in handling organization documents and explicit knowledge (information). This is set to change with information professionals transforming and bracing themselves for a more active and dynamic role in the information and knowledge society. At the same time, other professionals from other occupations and disciplines such as science, business, engineering, and information technology are also finding a niche in the information and knowledge management areas. These rapidly changing environments require diverse skills, new thinking, and broadened perspectives. Managing explicit and tacit knowledge within the organization is a challenging task. Tacit knowledge management requires dealing with the human elements that are closely related to human resource management, the appraisal system, the organization's culture, and its business practices. As organizations become aware of the value of keeping knowledge within the organization, they will require knowledge managers to manage knowledge within the organization and prevent its outward flow. Thus knowledge management goes beyond information management to include many other skills, competencies, cultural issues, organizational issues, and learning.

The increased emphasis on innovation, creativity, collaboration, and teamwork have influenced the job market and created the need for an interdisciplinary approach to knowledge management education. Knowledge professionals need to have a broader education that enables them to deal with a complex technological environment and the large amount of information generated every day, and that encourages and promotes knowledge-sharing activities to help ensure that information and knowledge acquired by the organization is utilized and translated into products and services.

Disciplines in support of knowledge management include information technology, information and library science, communication and cognitive science, business and management. The ability to derive a set of core modules from these disciplines is key to the establishment of knowledge management as a career.

In this book, the major issues in knowledge management, including intellectual capital, knowledge management technologies, knowledge sharing, organization culture, communities of practice, the learning organization, and knowledge management education, are discussed. The book provides a good reference text for a foundation course in knowledge management at both the graduate and undergraduate levels. It is also useful for people who would like to get an insight into the issues that concern knowledge management as a whole and information and knowledge professionals in particular. The first chapter provides an introduction to the changes taking place as a result of the move toward the knowledge economy. It highlights the importance of the national information infrastructure and its role in economic development and improving the quality of life. It also emphasizes the importance of education as a key to creating new knowledge, adapting to the fast-changing working environment, and dealing with the increase in the amount of information created every day.

The second chapter discusses the issues pertaining to the complexity of knowledge and the challenges most organizations face when it comes to managing knowledge resources. It attempts to differentiate between the different types of knowledge and the complexity involved in trying to manage them. While it is possible to codify the know-how and know-who, it is almost impossible to codify tacit knowledge in the form of skills and competencies. The best way of ensuring knowledge transfer in this area is through socialization and human interaction. The third chapter outlines the various components of intellectual capital and the various measurements used to account for intangible assets within the organization. Intellectual capital is closely linked to the knowledge activities that take place in the organization and the ability of an organization to leverage knowledge in its operations has a direct impact on intellectual capital and the worth of the organization.

Chapter 4 emphasizes the role of technology in knowledge management. While it is accepted nowadays that knowledge management is not merely about technology, technology plays an important role in facilitating knowledge management activity in the organization. Chapters 5–8 deal with the knowledge management issues that involve knowledge sharing, organization culture, communities of practice, and the learning organization. These issues are fundamental to the success of any knowledge management initiative within any organization. The last chapter focuses on knowledge management education and the need for an interdisciplinary curriculum that provides information and knowledge professionals with a broader education. As information and knowledge professionals are expected to assume higher responsibilities in dealing with the influx of information and oversee the management of the organization's knowledge resources and intellectual capital, they are expected to manage the process and ensure that business needs are served, to develop high-level knowledge management strategies and to establish a knowledge management infrastructure.

The knowledge management curriculum will continue to evolve, and as people from different disciplines come together and realize the importance of interdisciplinary education, a knowledge management discipline will emerge which eventually will help cultivate a new generation of information and knowledge professionals.

Acknowledgements

I would like to thank my family for their understanding and support during the long hours spent in the course of writing this book. I would also like to thank my colleagues and students for their participation in the informal discussions that contributed significantly to the ideas expressed in this work.

List of abbreviations

AI	artificial intelligence
APQC	American Productivity and Quality Center
BSC	Balanced Scorecard
CAP	Common Authentication Protocol
CEO	chief executive officer
CIO	chief information officer
CIV	current intangible value
CKO	chief knowledge officer
CMM	capability maturity model
COP	community of practice
CRM	customer relationship management
CTO	chief technology officer
DIC	direct intellectual capital method
EKP	enterprise knowledge portal
EVA	Economic Value Added
FC	financial capital
FIFARS	Federal Interagency Forum on Aging-Related Statistics
GDP	gross domestic product
GII	global information infrastructure
GIIC	Global Information Infrastructure Commission
GUI	graphical user interface
IAM	Intangible Assets Monitor
ICM	intellectual capital management
ICT	information and communication technologies
ICT	intellectual capital
IT	information technology

KBE	knowledge-based economy
KG	knowledge gap
KM	knowledge management
KMIM	knowledge management integrated measurement
KMM	knowledge management maturity model
KSS	knowledge structures and services
KVA	knowledge value added
LDAP	Lightweight Directory Access Protocol
MBA	Master of Business Administration
MCM	market capitalization method
NICI	national information and communication infrastructure
NII	national information infrastructure
OCR	optical character recognition
OECD	Organization for Economic Cooperation and Development
PARC	Palo Alto Research Center
PDA	personal digital assistant
R&D	research and development
ROA	return on assets
ROK	return on knowledge
SC	scorecard method
SECI	socialization, externalization, combination and internalization model
SMEs	small and medium-sized enterprises

List of figures and tables

Figures

Tables

About the author

Suliman Al-Hawamdeh is a professor in knowledge management at the University of Oklahoma in the US. He was the founder and director of the knowledge management program in Nanyang Technological University in Singapore and also the founder and president of the Information and Knowledge Management Society (iKMS). Dr Al-Hawamdeh has extensive teaching and working experience in areas such as knowledge management, electronic commerce, document imaging, information retrieval, the Internet, and digital libraries. He worked as a consultant to several private and government organizations and was the managing director of ITC Information Technology Consultants, a company specializing in imaging, document and drawing management products. Dr Al-Hawamdeh is the author of the book *Information and Knowledge Society* published by McGraw-Hill and is the editor in chief of the *Journal of Information and Knowledge Management*. He is also the editor of a book series entitled Knowledge Management and Innovation published by World Scientific.

The author may be contacted via the publishers.

The dawn of the knowledge economy

Introduction

Knowledge and innovation have played an important role in the development of society throughout history. The transformation from agrarian to industrial and now to the information and knowledge society has largely been brought about as a result of the accumulation of knowledge and the advances in information and communication technologies. Knowledge belongs to the individual, and building on it depends on other forms of knowledge, including information. Thus, rather like a set of building blocks, knowledge creation is a gradual process of adding value to previous knowledge through innovation. This implies that the more knowledge we generate and possess the more we are in a position to create and transfer knowledge to others. The key to economic success is always linked to the advances in knowledge creation and innovation and the ability to translate that knowledge into products and services.

But while knowledge as an economic driving factor has existed since the birth of mankind, it has only recently been recognized as a factor of production and attracted much attention. The recognition of knowledge as the driver of productivity and economic growth will lead to a new focus on the role of information and knowledge professionals and the importance of technology and learning activities. The term 'knowledge-based economy' stems from this recognition of the place of knowledge and technology in the new economy.

The term knowledge-based economy refers to the increased reliance on knowledge and innovation in the creation of products and services. According to the Organization for Economic Cooperation and Development (OECD), a knowledge-based economy (KBE) is one in which the production, distribution and use of knowledge are the main drivers of growth, wealth creation and employment for all industries. Governments are realizing increasingly that the way ahead in the developmental process lies in the progression to knowledge building and knowledge sharing. Neef (1999) pointed out that one of the main characteristics of the knowledge-based economy is the rapid pace of change that impacts our life and our society. Technologies are being altered, invented and thereafter deemed obsolete faster than ever before. Other characteristics include the rapid development and convergence of communications, computing and digital content which is enabling the current information revolution, including the Internet and the Web.

The liberalization of trade and global financial markets, the transfer of advanced operational technologies to developing nations, and the increased demand for knowledgeable and skilled workers are indications of the paradigmatic shift. As the flow of information is no longer inhibited by geographical boundaries, opportunities and threats that come along with the flow of information are impacting the transformation of society. For many organizations, it is no longer about pushing back the frontiers of knowledge but more about an effective use and exploitation of knowledge in all manner of economic activities.

The importance of the national information infrastructure

Countries around the globe are reviewing and restructuring regulations, financial operations and ownership in an attempt to take advantage of the knowledge-based economy. For many countries, moving to the knowledge economy requires establishing the foundation and infrastructure that will enable the transition to take place. For those countries which did not experience the Industrial Revolution, but have the means to leap into the knowledge society, heavy investment is required in the national information infrastructure (NII). The NII goes beyond the physical facilities which are used in the transmission, storage, and processing of information including voice, data, and images (Cordeiro and Al-Hawamdeh, 2001). NII encompasses a wide and expanding range of facilities that include equipment, policies and regulations, standards and – most importantly – people development. It ensures access to information and education, protects privacy and security, protects intellectual property, protects competition, and promotes technological innovation. An advanced NII will incorporate a seamless web of communication networks, computers, databases, and consumer electronics that will put vast amounts of information at a user's fingertips.

Governments can play a key role in the development of the national information infrastructure, especially in the areas of policies and regulation. Well-constructed government planning and policies enhance private sector organizations and enable them to play an active role in the development of the NII. A deliberate attempt on the part of the government to lay the foundations for the NII will not only promote private sector investment but also ensure that information resources are available to all at affordable prices, so individuals are able to gain access to information services and resources. The government's NII will also act as a catalyst in promoting technological innovation and new applications in various fields of work, promoting a seamless, interactive and user-driven operation of the NII.

The national information infrastructure benefits citizens through the establishment of community access networks and the dissemination of information that is crucial to the establishment of a democratic society as well as through narrowing the gap between economic advantage and disadvantage for various groups of people. The research community has always been recognized as being of paramount importance for a knowledge economy to exist and grow to become economically competitive. With a sound national information infrastructure in place and greater resources, researchers, through the use of knowledge-sharing and collaboration tools, are now able to share research information, access databases, share documents, and communicate their findings with colleagues.

The NII also provides the necessary infrastructure needed for lifelong learning as a key instrument in ensuring success in the knowledge economy. Just as corporations need to continuously upgrade the skills of their employees to keep them relevant, governments will also need to take care of long-term human capital development to sustain economic growth.

The national information infrastructure in developed countries such as the United States provides navigation through various sectors such as education, electronic commerce and government services. It provides access to integrated information and services, environmental monitoring, library services, electronic government information and world-wide digitized resources.

Michael Nelson, a keynote speaker in the Japan–US Information Infrastructure Symposium of June 1994 (CSIS, 1994), stated that, politically, the notion of advancing national information superhighways was set in motion when the Clinton Administration announced the establishment of a National Information Infrastructure (NII) initiative as a major policy. The NII is a system to deliver to all Americans the information they need when they want it and where they want it at an affordable price. The goal is to have 250 million channels, i.e. a channel for every American – a personalized channel for information and a two-way channel of information that provides interactive video throughout the country. But while the Clinton Administration, Congress and the Federal Communications Commission have outlined the rules and regulations for the NII, its success depends on American industry. This is because the major networks of telephones, broadcasting, cable and satellites launched in the US have been operated and owned by the private sector. However, the merging of information technologies has significantly increased the potential for electronic communications to facilitate broader social policy issues.

Many of the developing countries around the world have also realized the importance of the NII and the need to develop NII infrastructure capable of supporting the technological advances that might take place in each country. For example, increased recognition of the business and economic benefits of information and communication technologies (ICT) by African governments, the increase in the use of the Internet, and the launching of the African Information Society Initiative in 1996 are some of the practical steps taken toward the establishment of an NII infrastructure in Africa (*www.comnet-it.org*). Increased awareness by well-informed users and intense efforts by many of the development aid agencies have also fueled the development of national information and communication infrastructure (NICI) strategies in Africa. As African countries start to establish their own NICIs, experience has shown that the key challenge in building an information society in developing countries is securing institutional and political support at all levels. In many African countries, governments are more concerned with directing resources to essential activities like food production, health and education. Another important development in the African context is the establishment of the Global Information Infrastructure

Commission – Africa (GIIC Africa) that serves as the regional initiative of the Global Information Infrastructure Commission Forum (*www.giic.org/giicafrica*). GIIC Africa was launched in 1998 in Johannesburg, South Africa to contribute to the development of the African Information Society.

In Asia, the national information infrastructure is being tackled on many fronts, with countries like Singapore, Korea and Hong Kong taking a lead comparable to that of the United States and Europe. Other countries like Malaysia, Taiwan and China are progressing rapidly toward the establishment of a sound national information infrastructure. Singapore and Malaysia have seen very active government participation almost at every level with very little participation from the private sector (Chew and Al-Hawamdeh, 2001). Due to rapidly changing information technology and increasing international competition, alliances across national and regional borders have become an inevitable trend. According to Lü Xinkui (GIIC, 1995), while many Asian countries have made outstanding achievements in national information technology and information infrastructure, the Asian region as a whole still has a long way to go to achieve the levels of informatization in Europe and America. Xinkui calls for a common and joint effort by all Asian countries to work on an equal and symbiotic basis, helping each other out in terms of NII.

In Latin America, several countries have launched a national information infrastructure initiative (UNESCO, 2000). Chile is one of the pioneers in this area, its information society initiative being outlined in a document titled 'Chile Moving Toward the Information Society' ('Chile Hacia La Sociedad de la Información') while in Jamaica the initiative is entitled the 'National Strategic Plan for Information Technology'. In Brazil, the Ministry of Science and Technology formed a group called the 'Information Society Program in Brazil' which initiated activities in August of 1999 and the Program was officially launched by the President of Brazil in December the same year (*www.socinfo.org.br*). One year later, with the participation of more than 300 individuals in Brazil and overseas, the Green Book was launched which outlined the important areas considered relevant to the information society in Brazil, from R&D to applications, from the government to the private sector, and from advanced technologies to social impact.

By connecting countries across the globe, the global information infrastructure (GII) provides a vehicle for expanding the scope of these benefits on a global scale. By interconnecting local, national, regional and global networks, by creating a network complex and a global information marketplace, and by encouraging broad-based social discourse within and among countries, the GII extends beyond its simple hardware and software. It is a system of applications, activities, relationships, and information.

The Telecommunications and Informatics Division of the World Bank assists countries in deploying the information infrastructure and reviews opportunities, challenges and the role of governments in its development. James Bond, the Division Chief of the Telecommunications and Informatics Division of the World Bank examined the role of the Bank and other multilateral financing institutions in presenting the new Information and Development Initiative launched by the Bank (World Bank, 2001). The World Bank is a significant source of finance for infrastructure, private and public, in emerging economies. However, its role is not only as a direct source of funds but, with its financing infrastructure of lending and equity and guarantees, it is also a catalyst in attracting financing from other sources. The challenges put forward by Bond to obtain a global information infrastructure include, first of all, the lack of such an information infrastructure. Here the role of governments would be to ensure that the infrastructure gets built, not to build it themselves. The next challenge is the need for an effective regulatory and business environment, which means having a regulatory function that manages sector-specific issues such as frequency allocation, interconnection, tariffs and public service obligations. And, ultimately, the greatest challenge as Bond sees it is that of human capacity and culture, in which economic changes have to be integrated on human terms that respect the individual and empower the individual to make the most of the new paradigm.

Paradigm shift

One of the important aspects of the knowledge economy is the gradual shift from material goods to intangible goods. In 1947 in the USA, for example, agriculture, farming and manufacturing industries contributed approximately 8.5 percent and 26.9 percent respectively of total gross domestic product (GDP). By 1999, these percentages had dropped to just 1.3 percent and 16.1 percent respectively. Conversely, the percentage share of finance and service-related industries rose from 18 percent in 1947 to 40.6 percent in 1999 (US Department of Commerce GDP Release, 2001). The US Labor Bureau of Statistics projects that the top ten industries with the fastest employment wage and salary growth for the period 1998 to 2008 will come from service-related industries such as computer and data processing services (117 percent increase in employment over a 20-year period), health services (+67 percent) and residential care (+57 percent). The ten fastest growing occupations over the same period also include service-related jobs such as computer engineers (+108 percent) and computer support specialists (+102 percent) (US Bureau of Labor Statistics, 2001). Such trends are apparent across various sectors as developed countries head towards a knowledge-based economy. The nature of organizations within these countries and across the globe are altering both internally and externally, projecting themselves globally and becoming geographically decentralized. New regional agreements on tariff reductions coupled with limitations to relying solely on domestic market demand have driven many companies toward global extension and the development of cross-national and cross-border operations extending into networks that comprise vendors, outsourced agents, and international distribution channels.

With the shift in business focus and the increased emphasis on knowledge, organizations need to adapt to the changing markets and tap new opportunities. This affects the organization structure and forces it to be more flexible and effective in terms of management, employees, and infrastructure. While it might be difficult to find common standards and measurements for many of the elusive organizational concepts such as knowledge assets, leadership, competencies, and so on, these will remain the determining factors that distinguish one organization from another. Technology-driven organizations are at the forefront of the knowledge market today since they have the capability and flexibility to adapt to a market lacking in their traditional counterparts. They should be more innovative and react faster to the changes in the market by putting new technologies to work to counter competition. However, most of these organizations are undergoing changes in terms of their size, structure, and management style. Many of the small and medium-sized enterprises (SMEs) focusing on traditional competitive factors such as productivity, price and local market share have reduced the number of employees and tried to make larger investments in technology in the hope that they will enhance their productivity and become more competitive. Many of these organizations are capitalizing on current technologies to expand their services on a global scale with operations stretching across geographic regions. Technological advances in transport and logistics have revolutionized the speed and cost structure of delivering cargo by sea or air around the world, thus helping to increase global merchandise trade. In 1995, the combined value of cross-border trade in goods and services broke the $6,000 billion mark for the first time (World Trade Organization, Press/44, 1996).

Given the cultural resistance to change, knowledge management might not be an easy concept to implement. The biggest challenge for many organizations today is how to encourage their staff to share knowledge. Neef (1999) noted that the reason most often cited by employees preventing the sharing of knowledge is that the organizational culture limits their freedom to contribute to problem-solving outside of their narrow departmental spheres. One method of overcoming such organizational culture would be for organizations to develop internal knowledge networks, where consultants, colleagues, and individuals with similar interests and knowledge from around the firm meet in dedicated groups to discuss leading practices and the lessons learnt. Incentive and reward systems can also be used to encourage knowledge sharing. Incentive and recognition tend to be more effective when used as part of a people development strategy. Organizations will also have to manage advanced technologies in computing and telecommunications in order to create the structure necessary for effective internal knowledge management practices. This considerable undertaking involves planning and building as well as providing maintenance and support for both hardware and software, all within the financial constraints of the organization.

Productive learning

With the dawn of the knowledge economy, governments around the world have to wrestle with the fact that the move towards the knowledge economy might bring about employment problems since machines are gradually infiltrating what most would traditionally consider non-machine fields. Banking and finance are examples of what most would have considered traditionally non-computer related fields in terms of public transactions. Just a decade ago, most people would go to the bank for many of the simple transactions that are now conducted by automated teller machines, over the Internet, and by phone banking. Not only have information technology and the Internet which enable people to work on the move threatened white-collar jobs but also many traditional jobs will be affected by the rapid pace of innovation in scientific development. Advances in technology also affect the structure of employment at almost every level, enabling a remarkable growth in labor-saving devices. In the last decade, displacement of labor from the manufacturing sector was, in part, compensated by the growth of employment in the IT sector and information and knowledge-based services. For many of those affected, making the change to information and knowledge-based services requires a certain level of education that in the knowledge economy will most likely be continuous and ever changing.

To many countries with no natural resources, a global and competitive economy demands the effective utilization of labor as a means for survival. This means employment in high-value services and products so that such nations can work towards improving the living standards of their people. As such, at issue is not merely the utilization of labor but its effective utilization in relevant industries. The use of modern technology and the development of an educational infrastructure that produces an educated and trained labor force is becoming an increasingly important factor for economic growth (Al-Hawamdeh and Hart, 2002). Which technologies to acquire and which technologies to deploy are some of the issues that governments will have to deal with. With any competitive advantage gained likely to be brief given the rapidity with which new information technologies are being developed, significant economic success will be relative to how well a nation organizes its market to its advantage and the flexibility of its own market in response to global economics. This requires marketing skills, organizational innovations and an educated workforce.

In the knowledge economy, education is key to creating new knowledge, adapting to the fast-changing working environment, acclimatizing to new socio-political structures and dealing with the increasing amount of information created every day. Education in this case is a continuous process that starts with the basics and goes beyond the tertiary level to become a lifelong learning process. Technical training is also needed to build a strong labor force that is able to keep up with a constant stream of technological advances which compress product cycles and delivery times. Such education goes beyond the classroom as working and living environments provide the setting for a different kind of education and dissemination of knowledge (Luthy, 1998). The foundations for lifelong learning begin early with basic education that develops an individual's capability for learning, interpreting information and adapting knowledge to local conditions. Sound secondary- and tertiary-level education, especially* in engineering and the sciences, may help a nation produce effective engineers and scientists respectively. Apart from teaching advanced analytical skills, tertiary education also plays a role in creating groups of people who are able to monitor technological trends and who will then be able to assess the nation's relevance to and prospects in the global market, thus helping the nation develop an appropriate national technological strategy. Aggressive investment in tertiary education in numerous East Asian economies, for example, enabled these nations to support the new industries that provided the basis for later economic development and satisfied the demand for engineers and other highly skilled workers to sustain the nation's technological strategy.

Productive learning does not, however, only occur in the classroom but also outside of formal education since people continue to learn at work and through formal and informal training on the job. Training on the job equips workers with the experience they need for similar types of jobs and it gives them the opportunity to discover new methods of working and new ideas in the process, thus increasing each individual's capacities and enhancing their skills and competencies. Continual training of the labor force helps in general to lower the unit cost of production as it increases worker productivity and their ability to constantly discover better ways to use new technology. Governments as well as the private sector can play their part in encouraging the continual training of employees in various industries. Governments, for example, can consider decentralizing education to lend power to private organizations that specialize in educational needs and have knowledge of the best ways in which to achieve a nationwide outreach of education (Cordeiro and Al-Hawamdeh, 2001). It might not be necessary for governments to increase spending in working towards their educational goals, but rather to improve upon the quality and delivery of education using technology and innovative ideas. While the returns on education are high, many people are unable to grasp that opportunity due to financial constraints, so government subsidies for lower income groups for educational purposes could also be a strategy in working towards an educated and well-trained workforce. In developing countries, the opportunity cost of gaining an education may sometimes prove to be a problem given that the time spent on education equals lost wages or, in the case of females, a loss of time at home to take care of the household and look after children.

Advances in the means to deliver education such as e-learning, virtual classrooms, and distance learning have increased the opportunities for education and reduced the cost of adult learning outside of the traditional classroom setting. There is now an increased number of educational institutions that offer distance learning courses in a wide range of disciplines. Distance learning offers individuals a chance to pursue a higher level of education at flexible hours outside of campus grounds. Teachers also need to adapt to the new environment and be able to take advantage of the new tools in delivering quality education. E-learning as a vehicle of education not only opens up vast opportunities for adults who want to pursue an education off campus, but it also provides the workforce with an additional tool for upgrading labor skills outside the confines of geographic boundaries.

The new educational delivery tools facilitate more student-centered learning and expand the scope and content of the curriculum. The wide scope of multimedia and the Internet are creating a new paradigm in the delivery of learning. The e-learning environment allows for greater flexibility in which lectures can be linked to and retrieved whenever convenient. Courses can be recorded and transmitted anywhere via satellite or cable. Discussions between peers or with teachers can also be conducted online to clarify concepts and exchange the latest information.

With improved presentation software, the e-learning environment is also more interactive and richer with the inclusion of colored graphics, audio, video, and CD-Roms. Teachers in different geographical areas are able to work together and collaborate to produce learning materials or even conduct classes in a virtual classroom setting. Teachers can now have access to richer content over the Internet to prepare their teaching material or carry out research. The e-learning environment exposes teachers to a different methodology for teaching. Collaboration among students using collaboration tools, discussion, and chat rooms is an added value to students engaged in distance learning.

The increased numbers of students in tertiary institutions who juggle studying and employment commitments are potentially missing some of the structured lessons. E-learning allows them to fulfill their course expectations at their own pace and time as they can view course notes or videos online, regardless of time and location. With improved access to learning resources and the provision of flexible student support systems, e-learning also allows for a more flexible approach to teaching and the development of learning resources and experiences that cater to different learning styles (Franklin and Peat, 2001).

That said, there are problems and challenges that educational institutions and governments need to deal with. Students participating in e-learning must be self-motivated and disciplined as the monitoring of learning is more difficult. Many organizations around the world still value classroom-based learning over distance learning. Assessing the quality of e-learning is very difficult since teachers teach reactively by responding only to what the student has submitted to them online. Today, many educational institutions use e-learning to complement classroom learning and many do not see e-learning as a substitute. To monitor the progress of learning, teachers need to direct students to one of the test sites or examination centers. Should an examination centre not be available, teachers need to find some other way of testing to prevent cheating, such as assigning in-depth projects or essay writing (Trotter, 2001). Monitoring the progress of assignments may also pose some difficulties. Another problem most organizations and educational institutions engaged in e-learning need to resolve is the currency of information. As many courses and training materials are uploaded to websites, there is a need to continuously update that information and ensure that it is relevant. The archiving and preservation of learning material is another issue that can prove costly and difficult.

2

The complex nature of knowledge

Introduction

Dictionaries might not be the best place to start with when it comes to defining knowledge. But most dictionaries refer to knowledge as a perception of the truth or justified true beliefs. According to the Merriam Webster Dictionary, knowledge is 'the fact or condition of knowing something with familiarity gained through experience or association'. The Macquarie Concise Dictionary defines knowledge as 'the fact or state of knowing; perception of facts or truth; clear and certain mental apprehension'. While these definitions are philosophical in nature, they highlight the complex nature of knowledge. Davenport and Prusak in 1998 attempted to define knowledge in the context of experience, values, processes, practices and norms. They stated that:

> Knowledge is a fluid mix of framed experience, values, contextual information, and expert insight that provides a framework for evaluating and incorporating new experiences and information. It originates and is applied in the minds of knowers. In organizations, it often becomes embedded not only in documents or repositories but also in organizational routines, processes, practices, and norms. (Davenport and Prusak, 1998: 5)

There is no consensus on the definition of knowledge and it is very difficult to try and define something the existence of which most of the time we are not aware. Instead, it is more practical to focus on the processes that involve knowledge activities and see how these activities can be optimized. One of the powerful means of acquiring knowledge is through socialization and interaction (Denning, 2001; Cohen and Prusak, 2001; APQC, 2001). Knowledge in the form of skills and competencies is normally acquired through training, socialization and interaction with the environment. Knowledge embodied in documents does not necessarily translate into useful and usable knowledge unless it is read, digested, manipulated and communicated from one person to another. In other words, knowledge can only reside in the minds of people; once it is outside the human mind it is information. The process of transforming knowledge into information is called codification. But not all types of knowledge can be codified and captured. Knowledge in the form of skills and competencies can only be transferred from one person to another through training, socialization and interaction with people and the environment. According to Brown and Druguid (1998), knowledge is not the property of an individual but rather is held collectively by people working together. The 'know-how' is knowledge created out of practice and collectively shared by the workgroup.

The confusion that surrounds knowledge management today can be attributed largely to the complexity of knowledge and its relationship to information and data. Figure 2.1 shows the transition from data to information to knowledge to intelligence and finally to wisdom. While the transition from data to information is obvious, the transition from information to knowledge is not that obvious or easy to explain. This becomes even more difficult when we talk about codifying knowledge in which knowledge can be captured as information. While we are able to derive useful information from data and transform part of

Figure 2.1 **The transformation process**

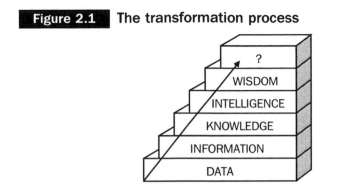

that information into knowledge, we are still not able to explain how these concepts relate to intelligence and wisdom. We also understand that not all types of knowledge can be derived from information. Tacit knowledge is a type of knowledge that is personal and which Polanyi (1958, 1966) referred to as something that we do unconsciously and most of the time we are not aware of its existence. Knowledge in the form of skills and competencies is normally acquired through training and interaction with the environment. It is not only difficult to articulate but, according to Polanyi, it is something that we cannot express and we do not even know. He explains, 'we can know more than we can tell'.

Obviously, not all types of knowledge are hidden and cannot be expressed. 'Know-how' and 'know-who' are types of knowledge that can be expressed and articulated (see Figure 2.2). A good example of the efforts to capture 'know-how' is the Xerox Eureka project (Bobrow, 1999). The Eureka system gathers shared tips on service repairs for technicians worldwide. The information captured in the system can benefit other technicians who might face the same or a similar problem. 'Know-how' in my opinion is what Nonaka and Takeuchi (1995) referred to when they talked about tacit knowledge to explicit knowledge conversion. According to them, knowledge conversion is about the interactions between explicit and tacit knowledge in a continuous spiral. Unlike skills and competencies, 'know-how' can be

Figure 2.2 Knowledge management

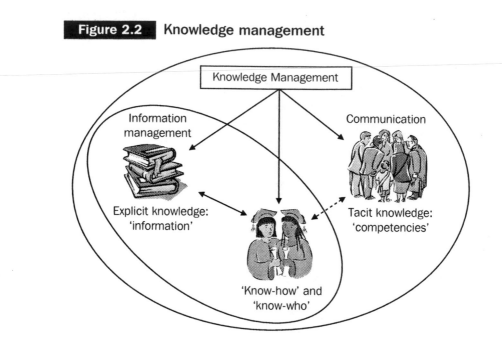

documented and the knowledge can be transferred through an independent learning process. This highlights the fact that not all types of knowledge can be captured and codified as information. A great deal of useful knowledge is normally lost when people leave an organization or feel that there is no incentive for them to share what is rightly theirs. In fact in the Eureka project, the biggest problem was motivating the service technicians to submit their tips. 'It took us a while to figure out the right incentive to get [the service technicians] to submit their tips,' says Dan Holtshouse, director of business strategy knowledge initiatives for Xerox, as quoted by the *CIO Magazine* in 1999.

Knowledge management

There is no accepted definition of knowledge management, largely due to the breadth of the concept and the complex nature of knowledge. Many believe that knowledge is personal, resides only in the minds of people, and most of the time we are not aware of its existence. Given that, managing knowledge in the same way as we used to manage information is neither logical nor practical. While information management is important and the need to manage digital information is greater than ever, information management is only a small part of knowledge management. Beside explicit knowledge (information), knowledge management includes 'know-how', 'know-who', and tacit knowledge. While 'know-how' and 'know-who' can be captured and documented as information, tacit knowledge can only be transferred through socialization and interaction.

Knowledge management can be viewed as the process of identifying, organizing and managing knowledge resources. These include explicit knowledge (information), 'know-how' (learning capacity), 'know-who' (customer capacity) and tacit knowledge in the form of skills and competencies.

Karl Wiig, a management consultant and practitioner, defined knowledge management as the systematic, explicit, and deliberate building, renewal, and application of knowledge to maximize an enterprise's knowledge-related effectiveness and returns from its knowledge assets (Wiig, 1999). Karl Sveiby, another consultant and one of the experts on intangible asset measurement, defined knowledge management as the art of creating value from an organization's intangible assets (*www.sveiby.com*). To him knowledge management consists of two tracks, the IT-track (management of information) and the people-track (management of people). The IT-track involves the construction of information management systems, AI, re-engineering, groupware, etc. The people-track involves people development, training, learning and managing competencies. According to the World Bank (2001), knowledge management is the management of knowledge through systematic sharing that can enable one to build on earlier experience and obviate the need for costly reworking of learning by making the same repetitive mistakes. De Long and Fahey (2000) looked at knowledge management from a business point of view and stated that the purpose of knowledge management is to enhance organizational performance by explicitly designing and implementing tools, processes, systems, structures, and cultures to improve the creation, sharing, and use of different types of knowledge (human, social, structural) that are critical for decision-making.

It is also important to emphasize the fact that knowledge management involves the management of explicit knowledge or information as well as the management of tacit and implicit knowledge in the form of skills and competencies. According to Davenport and Prusak (1998), knowledge management is concerned with the exploitation and development of the knowledge assets of an organization with a view to furthering the organization's objectives. Knowledge resources would include explicit knowledge in the form of captured or recorded information and tacit and implicit knowledge in the form of the expertise, skills and competencies of the people working in the organization. It also involves all of those processes associated with the identification, sharing, and creation of knowledge.

Knowledge management requires an infrastructure capable of supporting the creation and maintenance of knowledge repositories, and an environment that enables the cultivation and facilitation of knowledge sharing and organizational learning. Organizations that succeed in knowledge management are likely to view knowledge as an asset and to develop organizational norms and values which support the creation, retention, and sharing of knowledge.

Explicit knowledge refers to knowledge that can be expressed, captured, and documented in forms of publication such as trade secrets, patents, online databases, and so on. The ability to organize and manage explicit knowledge has a great impact on the other types of knowledge that are normally complex and associated with people. Implicit knowledge is knowledge that can be gained through learning and training. It is also a type of knowledge that can be self-acquired through reading and research. Tacit knowledge, on the other hand, is a hidden type of knowledge that is normally gained through socialization and interaction with the environment (see Figure 2.3).

Figure 2.3 Tacit knowledge

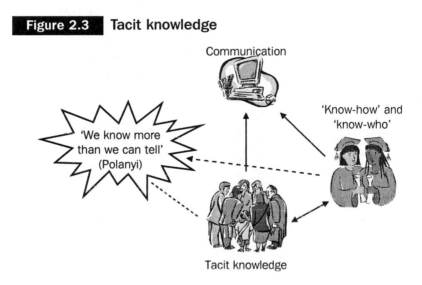

According to Nonaka and Takeuchi (1995), there are four types of interaction within and beyond an organization that are based on the distinct differences between tacit and explicit knowledge – socialization, externalization, combination, and internalization. The four interaction methods describe a dynamic process in which tacit and explicit knowledge are exchanged, transformed and converted. When an apprentice learns from his master, this form of learning is called *socialization* (from tacit to tacit). Socialization refers to the process of sharing tacit knowledge between people. This exchange of knowledge can take place in a one-to-one, one-to-many, or many-to-many interaction. Tacit knowledge can be transferred from one person to another without verbal or written documentation, for example via a shared experience and story-telling. Tacit knowledge can also be gained through observation, on-the-job training, and mentoring, and joint activities such as meetings and teaming up for a project. It deals mainly with communication and collaboration between people.

Externalization refers to the process of articulating and codifying tacit knowledge. It is the attempt to convert tacit knowledge into explicit knowledge. The process of externalization or codification involves the capture and documentation of tacit knowledge. Examples include documented standard operating procedures and periodic reports. 'Through conceptualization, elicitation, and ultimately articulation, typically in collaboration with others, some proportion of a person's tacit knowledge may be captured in explicit form' (Marwick, 2001). Externalization includes activities such as a discussion taking place among colleagues or team members, responding to a question and story-telling.

Combination refers to the process of converting explicit knowledge into more complex sets of explicit knowledge. Explicit knowledge can be shared and transferred via documents and e-mails. After an individual has accessed and retrieved the information, a reconfiguring process is likely to take place, whereby the information is sorted, understood and re-contextualized. In short, it deals with the processing of information (documented explicit knowledge). Placing a project report in the organization's shared repository is an example of the combination process.

Information technology has enabled the sharing and transfer of explicit knowledge or information in explicit-to-explicit interactions. The best example of a technology that facilitates explicit knowledge sharing is e-mail. E-mails enable people to communicate and exchange information almost instantly. Collaboration tools and groupware are also becoming common as a means to facilitate the transfer of explicit knowledge.

Organizations are increasingly turning to internal websites (intranets) and external websites (the Internet) in order to publish and distribute organizational knowledge, such as official organization documents, e-learning courses, guidelines, etc.

Internalization refers to the process of utilizing explicit knowledge. This requires processing external knowledge or information, understanding it, and then internalizing it. This, in turn, is supposed to create tacit knowledge for the individual. For example, internalization takes places when an individual accesses and reads a project report from the organization's shared repository, understands the report, and then contextualizes the information to suit his or her needs and own situation. This process depends on whether the individual can make sense out of the explicit knowledge. 'Successful internalization is a function of the sense-maker's individual attributes, including personal expertise, experiences, and mindset' (Junnarkar and Brown, 1997). Internalization can take place when an individual learns or gains knowledge by doing or via experience. Many practitioners disagree with this concept and refer to this process as 'know-how' creation rather than tacit knowledge creation.

It is important to look at knowledge management from the organizational point of view. Knowledge management caters to the critical issues of organizational adaptation, survival and competence in the face of increasingly discontinuous environmental change. Essentially, it embodies organizational processes that seek the synergistic combination of the data and information processing capacity of information technologies and the creative and innovative capacity of human beings (Malhotra, 1998). The Gartner Group refer to knowledge management as a discipline that promotes an integrated approach to identify, capture, retrieve, share, and evaluate an enterprise's information assets. These information assets may include databases, documents, policies, and procedures as well as tacit expertise and experience held by organization employees. Duffy (1999) states that knowledge management entails using methods to 'codify, capture, and make generally available the collective experiences of the organisation' – both tacit and explicit. This encompasses a combination of management awareness, attitudes and practices, systems, tools and techniques that enable knowledge to be shared and created.

Key drivers for knowledge management

For many organizations, knowledge management is a new concept. Although most organizations are engaged in various knowledge management practices, awareness of knowledge management and the need for doing it might not be that obvious. For many organizations, knowledge management is not about starting to do it but rather about how to do it better. So, then, what are the main incentives for any organization to focus on knowledge management? The following sections discuss some of the key drivers for knowledge management.

Achieving organizational efficiency

Knowledge management plays a significant role in achieving organizational efficiency. In the new economy, speed and responsiveness are determining success factors. Huang (1998) highlighted that responsiveness is a key to survival, including delivery of services, speed of implementation of global solutions and efficient processes. He added, 'Continuous improvement in operational efficiency and productivity is essential to long-term earning growth.' Indeed, in the Internet world where customers expect services to be available on a 24-hour basis, firms have no choice but to make a quantum-leap improvement in various aspects of their services such as time to market, time to solution and time to delivery or risk being forced out of business. This in turn has created the need for organizations to have organized information to facilitate their operations, information that is timely, accurate, useful and, more importantly, tailored to the organization's need. There is also increased pressure on firms to recycle and reuse knowledge instead of continually reinventing the wheel.

Staying ahead of the competition

In order to stay ahead of the competition, firms nowadays understand fully the need to know their customers and their competitors very well. Stewart (1997) recognized that customers are an integral part of the firm's intellectual capital. Many firms certainly understand the need to manage customers and IT solutions like customer relationship management (CRM) have proved to be highly popular. The other crucial factor in staying ahead of the competition is the need to know the competition. Lee, Wee and Bambang-Walujo (1991) highlighted that intelligence gathering/market intelligence is a crucial activity that companies must undertake in today's competitive business world.

Maximizing organizational potential

For many organizations, the main driver is maximizing the value of its R&D investments through 'recycling and reusing' experiments. Wakin et al. (1999) noted that companies like 3M and BP clearly understand the potential of knowledge management. For example, 3M prides itself on its ability to 'learn from mistakes' and also turn them into profitable products. Its Post-It note stickers are the epitome of such success through errors and has provided opportunities for cross-fertilization leading to successful spin-offs. The ability of an organization to innovate and create knowledge will depend largely on its ability to capture and manage knowledge. However, knowledge creation is an incremental process that requires the existence of a knowledge infrastructure. Knowledge management is about identifying and managing existing knowledge resources. It is also about making these resources available for knowledge workers to use in their work. Knowledge management professionals can play an important role in facilitating the knowledge creation process by facilitating knowledge-sharing and providing access to knowledge resources as and when these resources are needed.

Managing intellectual capital

In the knowledge-based economy, the value of an organization is largely measured by the value of its knowledge (or intangible) assets. Intellectual capital involves human capital, customer capital, structural capital and business intelligence capital. Each of these categories relies heavily on the creation and management of knowledge assets. Stewart (1997) highlighted the importance of knowledge when he stated, 'Knowledge has become the primary ingredient of what we make, do, buy and sell. As a result, managing it – finding and growing intellectual capital, storing it, selling it, sharing it – has become the most important economic task of individuals, business and nations.' He viewed *human* capital as the most important asset for companies nowadays and not the traditional view of raw materials and machinery. He noted that the way huge corporations scramble to find ways to retain their best staff (e.g. generous stock options, huge bonuses) is an indication. However, it is important to highlight that human capital on its own cannot make an impact. It needs customer capital and structural capital to enable the management of knowledge and intellectual capital within the organization.

Taxonomy of knowledge management strategies

The complex nature of knowledge and the inability to clearly define knowledge management opened the door for different knowledge management theories and strategies to evolve and the evolution of knowledge management practices and strategy will depend much on the approach used. So far, most knowledge management practices and strategies tend to swing between technology, business, and information science. Attempts to categorize knowledge management strategies provide guidance on the various approaches and tools available for knowledge management projects, as well as give a perspective on the taxonomy of knowledge management strategies. It is important to note that many of these strategies are theoretical.

Earl (2001) conducted case study research into six companies and came up with seven different knowledge management schools, stating: 'Each school is proposed as an ideal type. No claims are made that any one school outperforms others.' The first school is the *systems school*. The systems school focuses on the underlying technology and mechanism of creating knowledge bases for various processes or products. The knowledge bases comprise mainly custom and practice rules used in performing tasks such as machine calibration, decision-making, etc. They aim to codify tacit knowledge and encourage employees to document and share knowledge. This form of strategy requires certain technological support, especially in the form of knowledge-based systems.

The second school is the *cartographic school*. This school is concerned with knowledge mapping and the creation of taxonomies and knowledge directories. The maps or directories created are used as references to the knowledge and expertise that exist in the organization. Besides providing a key to the location of knowledge, such tools also aid organizations in identifying any inadequacy in their knowledge resources. Similar to systems schools technology plays an important role as it makes available profiles and directories on the Internet for people to refer to.

The third school is the *process school*. The process school, according to Earl (2001), is an extension of business process re-engineering. The school is also concerned with providing contextual and best-practice knowledge that will help business processes. The philosophy behind this school is to enhance the firm's core capabilities with knowledge flows supported by shared databases which can be accessed by all knowledge workers throughout a process.

The fourth school is the *commercial school*. In this school, an organization tries to maximize returns by capitalizing on its knowledge or intellectual assets. This could be in the form of patents, trade marks, copyrights, or know-how. Here, companies need to devise methods for the identification, assessment and protection of intellectual property. Information technology plays a secondary role in the the development and use of intellectual asset registration and processing systems.

The fifth school is the *organizational school*. This school is concerned with the organizational structure or networks such as discussion groups and communities of practices which facilitate the exchange and sharing of knowledge. Through knowledge communities, productivity can be increased as a result of knowledge reuse and accelerated learning. This can be enhanced by the use of technology in the form of collaboration tools, intranets, and portals.

The sixth school is the *spatial school*. This school is more concerned with the availability and accessibility of 'spaces' or channels that allow members of an organization to connect and share knowledge. The emphasis here is on the use of space that facilitates knowledge flows through the socialization process. Such 'spaces' can be a 'pantry' (knowledge café) or open-plan office where people can meet and share experiences and exchange ideas.

The seventh school is the *strategic school*. This school is concerned with the formulation of strategies using product, process, customer, and research knowledge to gain competitive advantage. As compared to the commercial school, the main aim of organizations under this school is actually to raise the consciousness level about value-creating possibilities available from recognizing knowledge as a resource.

From another perspective, Murray (2000) proposed eight organizational approaches that can be adopted for knowledge management. On closer examination, some of these eight approaches bear some similarities to the seven schools classified by Earl. These approaches include intellectual capital, knowledge as an individual skill, the philosophical approach, the technological approach, the teams and knowledge agents approach, the strategic approach, the process approach, and finally a combination of the previous seven approaches. However, some of these might overlap and therefore require a streamlining process. A combination of technology, process, and intellectual capital might prove to be useful to many organizations.

Beside the attempts by Earl and Murry to categorize knowledge management strategies, Mentzas (2001) classified knowledge management approaches into two categories: the product approach and the process approach. The product approach treats knowledge as an object which can be identified, processed and manipulated. Knowledge products can be packaged and transferred from one organization to another. The process approach focuses on the social aspect through communication and interaction. In the process approach, the development of communities is essential for knowledge management to succeed and the approach concentrates on the process of social communication to help generate knowledge.

Barclay and Murray (1997) identified three approaches to knowledge management. The first is the mechanistic approach characterized by the application of technology and resources. It uses networking technologies such as the Internet, intranets and groupware as knowledge management tools. The second category is the cultural/behavioristic approach which focuses on innovation and creativity. It also concentrates on developing organizational behaviors and culture. The third category is the systematic approach, which makes use of the rational analysis of the knowledge problem and tries to apply new thinking to old problems. It deems policies and work practices as important change agents and, as a result, believes that technology should be applied successfully to business knowledge problems themselves.

3

Intellectual capital

Introduction

The advances in information and communication technologies, the Internet and the Web have brought about the realization of the importance of knowledge and intangible assets. Intangible assets rely heavily on knowledge and the ability of an organization to translate that knowledge into products and services. The management of knowledge has been promoted as an important and necessary factor for organizational survival and the maintenance of competitive strength. The ability of the organization to identify knowledge resources such as intellectual capital and to manage these resources determines to a large extent the worth of the organization.

There is no generally accepted definition of knowledge or of a knowledge-based asset. Stewart (1997) viewed knowledge as a component of intellectual capital and has given a succinct definition of intellectual capital as 'packaged useful knowledge.' He explains that this includes an organization's processes, technologies, patents, employees' skills, and information about customers, suppliers, and stakeholders. Various other definitions use concepts such as ability, skill, expertise, and other forms of knowledge that are useful in the organization. Employees have long been recognized as an important and valuable resource by many organizations. The dictum 'our people are our main asset' is a familiar citation that emphasizes the value of people in an organization and highlights the importance of knowledge which resides in the minds of people. Normally, when people leave the organization, their knowledge leaves with them and that creates a concern in organizations where many of the products and services are knowledge based. One of the biggest problems facing most organizations today is how to manage employees and retain their valuable knowledge within the organization. Translating employees' knowledge into material gains is another challenge knowledge organizations face and as a result they are turning to knowledge management in the hope of finding clues as to how to deal with this challenge.

Given the realization of the value of people in the knowledge-based economy, the very livelihood of organizations depends upon recruiting the best people and encouraging them to leverage what they know in developing products and services. It is important for an organization to develop effective strategies to motivate their knowledge workers and highly skilled professionals and instil in them a sense of belonging and ownership. This requires a new approach to the fundamentals of organization management from the perspective of managing knowledge and accounting for intangible assets. The key point that corporations need to take note of is that their employees are assets and not simply view their salaries as a cost to the organization. This paradigmic shift in thinking is more and more about the return on human capital investment. According to Loh (2001) human capital is 'the accumulation of an individual's intellect, potential and commitment that contributes to the achievement of an organization's vision and goal.'

Economic value and the worth of the organization are no longer about physical assets. Instead the real value of the organization lies in its intellectual capital in the form of the knowledge and talent that each individual possesses. Given that, organizations have to rethink their current practices with regard to hiring and retaining good staff. The concept of treating employees as an investment means that employees' skills and competencies will need to be continuously upgraded and improved. Organizations should realize that every employee has his or her own talents, values and interests, and leverage and develop these skills to increase the company's knowledge base and boost labor productivity.

Retaining good employees means that the corporation needs to create an environment of trust. Without trust, knowledge transfer and knowledge sharing will not take place. Trustworthiness and recognition have to start at the top. Management need to engage employees at all levels in the decision-making process. One step toward creating an environment of trust is to instill the sense of belonging in the employees, and giving them a more active role in the future of the organization makes them feel they are making an important contribution to its success.

Intellectual capital components

There is no accepted definition of intellectual capital or the components that constitute it. While most practitioners and scholars seem to think that intellectual capital is comprised of human capital, customer capital and structural capital, others differ in their approach to and categorization of the components of intellectual capital. However, the general consensus is that intellectual capital is comprised of human capital, structural capital and customer capital. Human capital refers to the skills and competencies of the organization's employees and their capabilities in creating products and services and supporting customers. In addition to individual skills and competencies, human capital includes the dynamics of a learning organization in a changing competitive environment, its creativity, and its innovativeness. Structural capital refers to the organizational infrastructure and its ability to meet market needs. Infrastructure includes technology systems, company images, databases, patents, trade marks, the organizational concept, and documentation. Customer capital refers to people with whom an organization does business or to whom it provides services (see Figure 3.1).

Figure 3.1 Intellectual capital

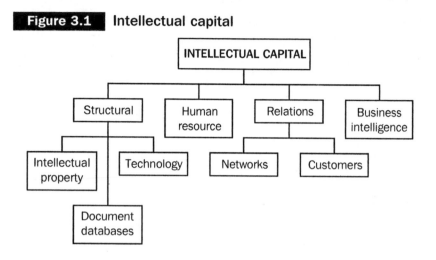

According to QBRonline.com, intellectual capital comprises human capital, organizational capital, market capital, and innovation capital. Market capital refers to the capabilities of an organization to interact with the external interface like the customer, partners, suppliers, and other stakeholders. Innovation capital refers to the organization's ability to innovate, improve, and develop unutilized potential as well as generate long-term wealth. Innovation capital is a new dimension although it could be argued that it is already included as part of human and structural capital. Brooking (1997), on the other hand, identified six components of structural capital or infrastructure assets. She listed financial relations as part of the structural capital. Clearly, while there is no general agreement among researchers and practitioners on what constitutes intellectual capital, there is a general consensus that intellectual capital consists of human capital, customer capital and structural capital.

Intellectual capital is closely linked to the knowledge activities that take place in the organization. It is the hidden value of the organization's knowledge that can be identified, acquired, retained, and utilized. Knowledge is not only associated with human, customer, and structural capital, but is also linked to the knowledge that can be acquired about competitors, the marketplace, products, and services which can be used to generate revenue and benefits to the organization. The ability of an organization to leverage knowledge in its operations has a direct impact on intellectual capital and the worth of the organization. But linking intellectual capital to organization knowledge might be difficult to conceptualize, especially when most of that knowledge resides in the mind of people who might leave the organization and take part of that knowledge with them. This is precisely why organizations today are interested in knowledge management in an attempt to protect the organizational assets.

The difficulty in dealing with organization knowledge is not new. For example, human capital is embedded in the organization in a form of tacit knowledge or know-how. It is difficult to capture or document tacit knowledge but organizations need to realize the importance of human capital and make an effort, first to retain good employees in the organization for a longer period of time, and second to make sure that the employees' knowledge is utilized and shared with other people in the organization. Encouraging knowledge sharing and knowledge transfer between people within the organization is one way an organization can effectively manage human capital. Encouraging staff to participate in seminars, workshops and continuous education is another way of enhancing the human capital within the organization

Customer capital or relationship management consists of business transactions, customer satisfaction and the value of customer feedback. Customer capital is relatively easier to capture as opposed to human capital. Some performance indices can be used to measure customer capital, for example repeat business transactions, market dominance due to market strategy, customer feedback and so on. In order to capture customer capital, it is a prerequisite to have a comprehensive database to capture business transactions. New technologies such as data warehousing and data mining tools are used to generate these performance indices.

Customer relationship management (CRM) is a growing area. New and improved technologies to facilitate CRM are capable of tracking and managing customer profitability, behavior and satisfaction at a reasonable cost. CRM is critical to corporate success in today's increasingly competitive environment (Anton, 1996). Delivering high-quality service and achieving high customer satisfaction have been closely linked to profits, cost-savings and market share. To retain customers, it is important for organizations to have a stronger focus and the ability to measure and manage the individual customer relationships.

Structural capital consists of manuals, databases, procedures and company culture and practices. These are the technologies, methodologies and processes that enable an organization to function. For example, a company could have a comprehensive information system that uses many computer-based applications such as financial systems and material management systems, etc., information from which is transmitted over a network infrastructure.

Another important area in intellectual capital is the organization's ability to deal with competition. Knowledge about competitors, their marketing strategy, product information and technology deployed has a great impact on the value of the organization. You could refer to this as business intelligence capital. This also involves the ability of the organization to make sense out the large amount of information collected over a long period of time. Technology plays an important role in providing tools to monitor the market, gather competitive information about competitors' products and services and analyze the existing large amount of data.

Intellectual capital measurement

Today, the market value of an organization can be considerably higher than the book value. This is particularly true in the case of knowledge-intensive companies such as information technology, e-learning, consultancy and so on. The increased emphasis on intangibles created a growing interest in how organizations measure and manage their intangible assets. Kaplan and Norton (1996) developed the Balanced Scorecard which is designed to focus managers' attention on the factors that help the business strategy and adds alongside financial measures of the customer, internal processes and innovation. Stern Stewart & Co., a consulting firm based in New York, introduced the concept of Economic Value Added (EVA) as a measurement tool in 1989. Stern Stewart & Co. proposed the EVA to assist corporations in pursuing their prime financial directive. While playing an important part, critics argue that they are static measures and do not help managers identify the underlying cause and effect. The lack of adequate practical measures has resulted in the development of new kinds of measures that could help in understanding and assessing an organization's intellectual capital. Examples of such measures include the Skandia Navigator and Karl-Erik Sveiby's Intangible Assets Monitor.

The issue of how to measure intangible assets and intellectual capital is still being explored by organizations, researchers, and management consultants. Most of the solutions available today are geared towards the measurement of both intellectual capital and intangible assets. Most of the measures proposed in the literature seem to fall into four categories:

■ *Direct intellectual capital methods (DIC)*. These look at the dollar value of intangible assets by attempting to identify the various components of intellectual capital.

- *Market capitalization methods (MCM).* These calculate the difference between a company's market capitalization and its stockholders' equity as the value of its intellectual capital or intangible assets.
- *Return on assets methods (ROA).* These link the earnings or the increased value of the organization to the cost and expenditure.
- *Scorecard methods (SC).* These are similar to direct intellectual capital methods except that no estimate is made of the dollar value of the intangible assets.

Direct intellectual capital methods

Direct intellectual capital (DIC) methods are based on measuring the dollar value of intellectual capital by identifying its various components. The problem with such an approach lies in the difficulty of identifying the various components of intellectual capital. Some of the components that can be identified include customer loyalty, patents, technology assets such as know-how, human assets such as education and training, and structural assets such as information systems. Once some of the components can be identified, they can be directly evaluated, either individually or as an aggregated coefficient. Examples of such methods include the technology broker and citation-weighted patents.

Technology broker

Brooking (1996) proposed the technology broker measurement, which offers three measurement models to help calculate the dollar value of intellectual capital. She divided intellectual capital into four different components (see Figure 3.2): market assets, human-centered assets, intellectual property assets, and infrastructure assets. Market assets refer to intangibles that are related to the organization's marketing efforts such as brand

Figure 3.2 Technology broker

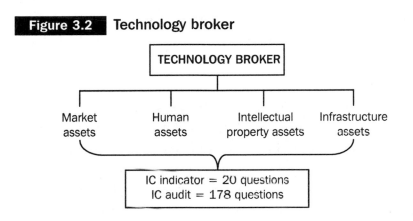

names, customers and customer relations, repeat business, distribution channels and so on. Human-centered assets refer to the skills and competencies, expertise, innovativeness, creativity, problem-solving capabilities and leadership, entrepreneurial and managerial skills of the employees in the organization. Intellectual property assets refer to patents, trade marks, copyrights, trade secrets and so on. Infrastructure assets involve technologies, methodologies and processes which enable the organization to function; it also includes the corporate culture, methodologies for assessing risk, methods of managing the sales force, the financial structure, any databases of information on the market or customers and the communication systems.

Brooking uses 20 questions as a start to assess the organization's intellectual capital. The fewer of the 20 questions the company is able to answer the more it needs to focus on its intellectual capital. In addition to the 20 questions that make up the IC indicators, each component of the technology broker is then examined further by another set of questions. The technology broker intellectual capital audit is made up of 178 questions. For example, the IC audit for human assets comprises five questions on employee education, five on vocational audit, twelve on work-related knowledge, eight on occupational assessment, eight on work-related competency, ten on corporate learning and three on human-centered asset management.

The citation-weighted patents

Bontis (1996) used the example of Dow Chemical to explain how patents can be used as proxies for practical IC measurement. A significant component of Dow's initial management of intellectual assets has been its review of patent maintenance within its research and development with the objective of creating cost-savings for the organization. The Dow model takes into account the steps leading to the creation of patent or intellectual property. This involves the cost of research and development and uses indicators such as research and development expense per sales dollar, number of patents, income per research and development expense, cost of patent maintenance per sales dollar and project life-cycle cost per sales dollar. Bontis (2001) emphasized that the 'patent evaluation process' is a team-based effort where members from R&D and marketing interact directly with production to decide whether the intellectual property is valuable. This involves accounting for intellectual property either by assigning value to the idea, abandoning it or writing it off as any other depreciated asset within the organization.

Patents are the most obvious form of intellectual capital and easy to control and account for. By using patents, Dow is able to measure the internal operations that lead to the creation of the intellectual property in the organization.

Market capitalization methods

Market capitalization methods (MCM) calculate the difference between an organization's market capitalization and its stockholders' equity as the value of its intellectual capital or intangible assets. While this sounds easy, the problem lies in determining the organization's market capitalization. To accurately calculate market capitalization, the historical financial statements must be adjusted for the effects of inflation or replacement costs. Examples of such methods include Tobin's q and market-to-book value.

Tobin's q

James Tobin, a Nobel Prize-winning economist, developed a measure, q, to help predict investment decisions. Tobin's q is essentially the same as the market-to-book ratio except that Tobin's q uses the replacement cost of tangible assets rather than their book value in the calculation (Luthy, 1998). Federal Reserve Chairman Alan Greenspan noted that high q and market-to-book ratios for a corporation can reflect the investments in technology (Stewart, 1997). Tobin's reasoning is based on the premise that a company is unlikely to buy more of an asset when that asset is worth less than its replacement cost. Conversely, a company is likely to invest if an asset is worth more than its replacement cost.

Tobin's q is calculated as the value of a firm's capital divided by its replacement cost. If $q < 1$ it is not good to invest. If $q > 1$, it is good to invest. The ratio is an improvement over other market-to-book measures that simply view intellectual capital as just the difference between a company's market value and its book equity. The attractiveness of Tobin's q model is that it has the advantage of a market-to-book ratio while also saying something about the effect of diminishing returns. Stewart believes Tobin's q is considered applicable not just for assets but for company assets as a whole. It is considered capable of neutralizing different depreciation policies and is most informative when companies are compared over a long period of time. The main weakness of the measure is the difficulty in quantifying replacement costs, making it difficult to apply.

Market-to-book value

The general idea of a market-to-book ratio is to determine what value the stock market gives a company compared with the value of the company as indicated on the company's balance sheet (Stewart, 1997). In other words, it measures the difference between the physical book value of an asset and its market valuation. The difference is then attributed to the intangible value of the intellectual capital which is not captured by the traditional accounting system. The market-to-book ratio is equal to the price per share divided by the book value per share.

According to Stewart, this measure by itself has limited value for several reasons. First, stock prices are affected by many economic factors not associated with a company's tangible or intangible assets, and secondly, book values represent depreciated historical costs that rarely coincide with the 'true' value of revenue-generating tangible assets. Although fluctuation in the stock price can indirectly affect the overall value of the organization, it is not a good indicator of the worth of the organization in terms of intellectual capital. Stock values do fluctuate and are influenced by external factors, which might not be related to the otherwise sound foundations and capabilities of the organization.

Return on assets methods

The return on assets (ROA) model calculates the average pre-tax earnings of a company for a period of time and divides it by the average tangible assets of the company over the same period of time. The resulting ROA is compared with the company's industry average to calculate the difference. If the difference between the company's ROA and its industry average is positive, then the company is assumed to have excess intellectual capital over its industry. This excess ROA is then multiplied by the company's average tangible assets to calculate an average annual excess earning. By dividing the excess earnings by the company's average cost of capital or an interest rate, we can derive an estimate of the value of its intangible assets or intellectual capital. Examples of such a method include Economic Value Added and calculated intangible value.

Economic Value Added

As noted earlier, the Economic Value Added model was introduced by Stern Stewart & Co. in 1989 as a tool to assist corporations in pursuing their prime financial directive by aiding in maximizing the wealth of their shareholders (Bontis et al., 1999). According to Stewart, EVA is the financial performance measure that comes closest to capturing the true economic profit of an enterprise.

The EVA equation (Horngren, Foster and Datar 1997) is as follows:

$$\text{EVA} = \frac{\text{After-tax}}{\text{operating income}} - \left[\frac{\text{Weighted average}}{\text{cost of capital}} \times \left(\frac{\text{Current}}{\text{liabilities}} - \frac{\text{Total}}{\text{assets}}\right)\right]$$

where the weighted average cost of capital (WACC) equals:

- the after-tax average cost of all the long-term funds used by the company;

and total assets minus current liabilities equals:

- Long-term assets + Current assets − Current liabilities; or
- Long-term assets + Working capital.

In order to have a positive EVA, an organization's rate of return on capital, which is equal to the organizational income divided by its investment, must exceed its required rate of return. According to Bontis (2001), EVA is a very complex system to implement and involves more than 164 different areas of performance adjustment. The use of book assets relies on historical costs which give little indication of current market or replacement value. Bontis states that empirical research has not shown conclusively that EVA is a better predictor of stock price or its variation.

Calculated intangible value

Calculated intangible value (CIV) uses the average pre-tax earnings of a company for a period of time. This average earning is then divided by the average tangible assets of the company over the same period of time. The resulting ROA is compared with the company's industry average to calculate the difference. Stewart (1995) discusses how it can be applied to the measurement of intellectual capital. He provides a seven-step process for ADAK Laboratories to use:

1. Calculate average pre-tax earnings for the past three years.
2. Go the balance sheet and get the average year-end tangible assets for the same three years.
3. Divide earnings by assets to get the return on assets.
4. For the same three years, find the industry's average return on assets (ROA).
5. Calculate the 'excess return'. Multiply the industry-average ROA by the company's average tangible assets. Subtract that from the pre-tax earnings in step 1.
6. Calculate the three-year-average income tax rate and multiply this by the excess return. Subtract the result from the excess return to get an after-tax figure – the premium attributable to intangible assets.
7. Calculate the present value of the premium by dividing the premium by an appropriate discount rate such as the company's cost of capital.

According to Luthy (1998) calculated intangible value does not have the precision of other balance sheet numbers but is useful in a number of ways. It can be used as a benchmark measure in that calculated intangible value could help ascertain whether an organization has value not reflected in traditional financial measures. It can also be used by management in that a strong or rising calculated intangible value could be seen as an indicator that their investment in knowledge assets is working.

Scorecard methods

The scorecard model identifies the various components of intangible assets. The indicators and indices are generated and reported in scorecards or as graphs. The scorecard methods are similar to direct intellectual capital methods except that no estimate is made of the dollar value of the intangible assets. A composite index may or may not be produced. Examples of such methods include the Skandia Navigator, the IC Index, the Intangible Assets Monitor and the Balanced Scorecard.

The Skandia Navigator

The 'Navigator' developed by Swedish firm Skandia is one of the best-known business models developed to identify intangible assets considered critical to company performance. Skandia has for a number of years issued intellectual capital reports as supplements to its annual reports (Edvinsson and Malone, 1997). The Navigator is a reporting model that shows a balanced picture of Skandia's financial and intellectual capital, and is based on the same broad conceptual framework as the 'Intangible Asset Monitor'. It is designed to provide a balanced picture of financial and intellectual capital. The framework focuses on five areas with Human Focus at the heart of the process (see Figure 3.3). The five areas comprise Financial Focus, Customer Focus, Human Focus, Process Focus and Renewal and Development focus.

Figure 3.3 The Skandia Navigator

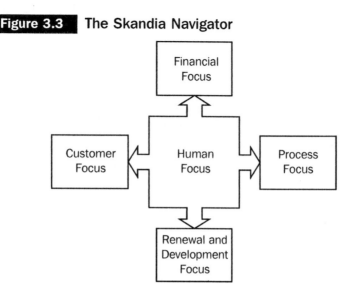

The Financial Focus is added to the broader intellectual capital focus to provide the historical financial perspective. The Process Focus refers to the organization's internal structure including patents, concepts, models, and computer and administrative systems that are created by the employees and are generally owned by the organization. The Customer Focus refers to the organization's external structure and includes relationships with customers and suppliers. The Renewal Focus includes measures that indicate how well an organization is preparing itself for the future, for example the rate of new product design, the efforts to develop new markets, and a description of new management practices that will help the organization operate more effectively in the future. The Human Focus, which is placed at the centre of the model, refers to the skills, competencies and capability of the people in the organization.

The implementation of the Skandia Navigator involves 164 metric measures (91 intellectually based and 73 traditional metrics) that measure the five areas of focus making up the Navigator model. According to Edvinsson, the corporate director of intellectual capital for Skandia, the metrics use direct counts, dollar amounts, percentages, and survey results to produce two types of measurement: monetary and percentage measurements. Monetary measures are combined using a pre-determined weighting to produce an overall intellectual capital value for the organization; the percentages are combined to produce the coefficient of intellectual capital. The overall intellectual capital is then calculated by multiplying the overall value with the coefficient of intellectual capital.

Intellectual Capital Index

The Intellectual Capital Index (IC Index) was developed by Goran and Roos of the London-based firm Intellectual Capital Services Limited in 1999 (see Figure 3.4). It attempts to consolidate the various IC indicators to form a measurement that can dynamically describe intellectual capital and its development over time. The conceptual base draws upon a broad base of theory including the resource-based view of the firm, competency models, performance models including the Balanced Scorecard, the Skandia Navigator, knowledge categories, and strategic value analysis (Roos et al., 1997). The IC Index was developed to help managers visualize the growth or decline in capital and also the trade-off.

Intangible Assets Monitor

The Intangible Assets Monitor (IAM) was developed by Karl-Erik Sveiby, one of the pioneers in the development of intangible asset measurements (*www.sveiby.com*). This method divides the intangible assets of an organization into three components: external structure, internal structure and employee competence. Management selects indicators, based on the strategic objectives of the firm, to measure the four aspects of creating value from intangible assets: growth, renewal, utilization/efficiency and risk reduction/stability.

Figure 3.4 Intellectual capital tree as proposed by Goran and Roos

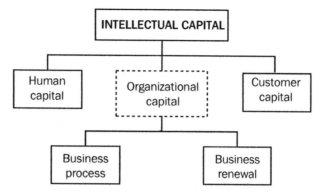

Sveiby recommends the use of both financial and non-financial measures to provide a complete indication of financial success and shareholder value (see Figure 3.5). The intangible assets framework is categorized into three different indicators:

Figure 3.5 Intangible Assets Monitor (after Sveiby)

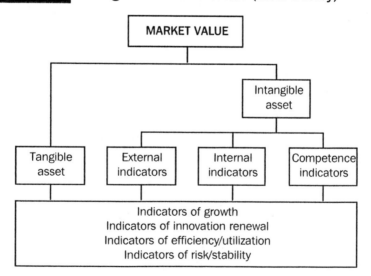

External structure indicators

This consists of relationships with customers and suppliers, organization image and reputation, brand names and trade marks. Customer relation management and the ability to understand the market reflect on the value of the organization. While these are of great value to the organization, some are difficult to quantify or assess. For example, the image and reputation of the organization can change over time and are sometimes wrongly perceived.

Internal structure indicators

This consists of patents, concepts, models, and computer and administrative systems. The internal structure also includes information systems, databases, investment in IT, and any other infrastructure that supports the organization's activities. It also includes culture and internal social networks. In the knowledge management environment this also include communities of practice within the organization, best practices, and any other processes that contribute to the success of the organization.

Individual competence indicators

This refers to people capacity and their abilities to deliver and perform. It includes skill, education, experience, values, and social skills. Human capital is the focus for many intellectual capital measurements. The knowledge which resides in people's minds cannot be owned by any organization but is a critical component in determining the value of the organization. The ability of the organization to leverage that knowledge and transform it into products and services is what can be considered intellectual capital.

Balanced Scorecard

Kaplan and Norton developed the Balanced Scorecard (BSC) in the early 1990s as part of a one-year project sponsored by the

Nolan Norton Institute, the research arm of KPMG. The findings of the study, titled 'The Balanced Scorecard – measures that drive performance', were first published in the *Harvard Business Review*, January–February 1992. The Balanced Scorecard is designed to take a more balanced view on internal performance measurements. Kaplan and Norton (1996) suggested that managers need a multi-dimensional measurement system to guide their decisions: a Balanced Scorecard including leading and lagging indicators and measurements focusing on the outside and inside of the company.

The Balanced Scorecard gives managers information from four different perspectives, while minimizing the number of measures used. The four different perspectives are illustrated in Figure 3.6, which revolves around the organization's vision and strategy. In fact the objectives and measures of the Balanced Scorecard are derived from the organizational vision and strategy. The four perspectives are financial, customer, internal business process, and learning and growth. The financial perspective includes traditional accounting measures such as growth rate, shareholder value, and company profitability. The customer perspective measures relate to the identification of target groups for the company's products in addition to marketing-focused measures of customer satisfaction, retention, etc. Excellent customer satisfaction derives from the processes, decisions, and actions occurring throughout an organization. The internal business process perspective focuses on those critical internal operations that enable managers to satisfy customer needs. The innovation and learning perspective includes all measures relating to employees and systems the company has in place to facilitate learning and knowledge diffusion. The Balance Scorecard uses a set of cause–effect relationships that form a network of linked indicators. It is a comprehensive framework that translates the company's strategic objectives into a coherent set of performance measures which span the four different perspectives. The process

Figure 3.6 **The Balanced Scorecard**

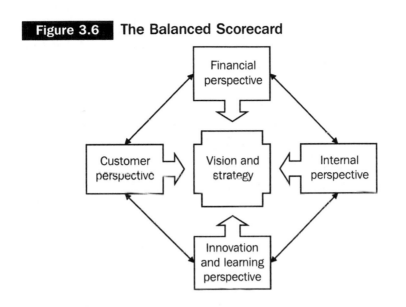

of building a Balanced Scorecard requires a reinterpretation of long-term strategy through the lenses of the four perspectives.

Knowledge management measurements

Intellectual capital measurements are mainly concerned with measuring intangible assets and the dollar value of an organization. They deal with the various components of intellectual capital such as human capital, customer capital, and structural capital. Knowledge management measurements look at the wider picture and take into consideration other important issues such as knowledge gaps and the effectiveness of knowledge management programs.

Intellectual capital measurements can be viewed as accounting and auditing practices attempting to account for the intangible assets that, when added to the tangible assets, make up the total value (market value) of the organization. In non-profit organizations, the measurement of intangibles in terms of dollar value might not be that important. Instead, non-profit organizations are mainly concerned with the quality of services and the effectiveness of managing resources and expenditure. Knowledge management measurements therefore need to go beyond intellectual capital measurements and include other components such as performance issues, knowledge-sharing activities, and knowledge gap assessments.

One of the methods proposed in the literature for assessing the effectiveness of knowledge-management implementations is the return on knowledge (ROK) approach (Housel and Bell, 2001). Some of the proposed measures in this category include the knowledge value-added (KVA) methodology and knowledge structures and services (KSS). KVA provides a methodology for allocating revenue and cost to an organization's core processes based on the amount of change each organization produces. KSS on the other hand provides a way to characterize knowledge management tools by defining the types of knowledge they can handle and the types of services they provide to support knowledge management processes.

Another model proposed by Kochikar and his team at Infosys Technologies Inc. is the knowledge management maturity model (KMM). KMM can be used to assess the relative maturity of an organization's knowledge management effort (Kochikar, 2000). The model is based on SEI's capability maturity model (CMM) and defines five knowledge management maturity levels: default, reactive, aware, convinced, and sharing. Each maturity level can be characterized by certain observable capabilities along each of the three major prongs: people, process, and technology. The problem with the existing knowledge management models is that they provide a partial assessment and focus only on certain aspects of knowledge management. They also lack the formulae or the criteria needed by the organization to be able to assess the effectiveness of knowledge management practices over a certain period of time.

Knowledge management integrated measurement model

The knowledge management integrated measurement model (KMIM) focuses on the effectiveness of knowledge management practices within the organization. KMIM assesses the knowledge management effectiveness factor within the organization using four different components. The first component is the intellectual capital, which looks at human capital, customer capital, and structural capital, and for the first time includes business intelligence capital. The second component is financial capital. Financial capital is the tangible asset component that has a direct impact on the execution of any knowledge management activity such as learning processes and training. The third component is performance and knowledge-sharing activities at the individual as well as the group level. By including knowledge-sharing activities in the performance component, organizations can create the needed incentives for employees to share knowledge. The fourth component in KMIM is assessment of the knowledge gaps within the organization. The existence of knowledge gaps within the organization can be attributed to many factors, including learning curves, a loss of expertise or talent as a result of people leaving the organization, an inability to do the job due to lack of training and knowledge sharing, and so on. In the case of staff leaving the organization, the knowledge gap can be assessed by the cost of training new staff to do the job plus the loss in productivity resulting from the original staff leaving the job. Figure 3.7 shows the relationship between the four components that can be used to determine the KMIM effectiveness factor.

Intellectual capital

KMIM recognizes the importance of business intelligence and the need to incorporate it as part of intellectual capital. Knowledge about the marketplace, competitors, and their products and

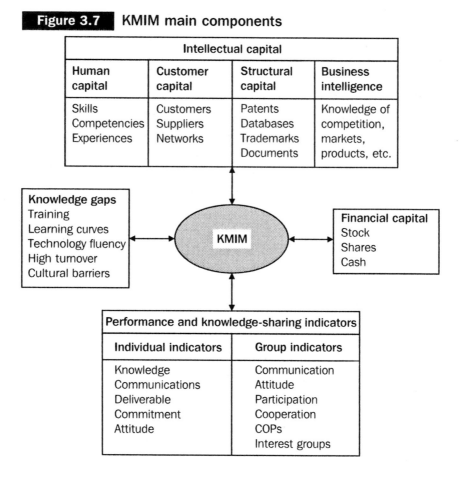

Figure 3.7 KMIM main components

Intellectual capital			
Human capital	**Customer capital**	**Structural capital**	**Business intelligence**
Skills Competencies Experiences	Customers Suppliers Networks	Patents Databases Trademarks Documents	Knowledge of competition, markets, products, etc.

Knowledge gaps
Training
Learning curves
Technology fluency
High turnover
Cultural barriers

KMIM

Financial capital
Stock
Shares
Cash

Performance and knowledge-sharing indicators	
Individual indicators	**Group indicators**
Knowledge Communications Deliverable Commitment Attitude	Communication Attitude Participation Cooperation COPs Interest groups

services enables the organization to make better decisions and stay ahead of the competition. Intellectual capital in KMIM includes human capital, customer capital, structural capital, and business intelligence. Some of the intellectual capital measurements discussed earlier such as the Intangible Assets Monitor and Balance Scorecard can be used to assess the intellectual capital component in KMIM. However, these measurements do not include business intelligence and there is a need to incorporate it as part of the intellectual capital assessment.

Financial capital

Effective knowledge management practices should also result in a better management of the organization's financial resources. Financial capital combined with intellectual capital results in the dollar value (market value) of the organization. While the market value of the organization gives an idea of the overall organizational performance, it does not tell us much about the effectiveness of knowledge management in various departments within the organization. Some departments within the organization could be doing very well and contributing to the overall performance whereas other departments are performing poorly.

Performance and knowledge-sharing indicators

Integrating knowledge-sharing activities as part of the employee performance process at the individual as well as the group level provides the needed incentive for knowledge-sharing to take place. Staff participation in knowledge-sharing activities such as interest groups, discussion forums, projects, communities of practice, focus groups and informal networks is an indication of their willingness to share and learn and at the same time contribute to the organization's knowledge value. Incorporating these activities into the overall employee performance process sends a clear message that knowledge contributions and time invested in knowledge-sharing activities pay off. KMIM takes performance and knowledge-sharing activities into account and uses them to measure the effectiveness of knowledge management practices within the organization. Performance indicators can also be used to measure the extent by which an organization is able to leverage the skills and competencies of its human resource capital. Placing a value on the competencies, skills and experiences of its employees is one thing but the ability to translate those skills and competencies into products and services is another. The organization's investment in training and learning needs to be translated from a cost to the organization to either a profit or a service to the community depending on the organizational goals and objectives.

Performance and knowledge-sharing activities can be monitored at the individual and the group level. At the individual level, indicators such as consistent performance, attitude, ability to meet deadlines, alertness, conceptualization skills, and proactiveness can be used. At the group level, indicators such as the ability to work within groups, leadership role, attitude, contribution, and participation at different levels can be used. Knowledge-sharing activities can be monitored using participation in group discussions, interest groups, communities of practice, learning activities, seminars, conferences, etc.

Knowledge gaps

The ability to identify knowledge gaps within the organization is in itself a knowledge management activity. The ability of an organization to learn from past experiences and adjust itself to the changing environment requires a constant monitoring of the knowledge gaps within the organization. For example, when an organization decides to embark on a simple task like starting a training program, there should be a knowledge gap assessment to determine the usefulness of such a program. The identification of knowledge gaps enables the organization to design effective and efficient programs and initiatives. Figure 3.7 lists some examples of the knowledge gaps that can be identified within the organization. 'Learning curves,' for example, refer to the knowledge gap that occurs within the organization when an expert decides to leave. The time needed to recruit someone and the time taken to train the new member of staff is considered a knowledge gap. Organizations need to look beyond the cost factor when it comes to training and learning activities within the organization. While there is a cost involved in training and retraining staff for specific jobs, there is a bigger loss in productivity and output as a result of staff leaving the organization. The longer the training takes or the steeper the learning curve is, the greater the cost and the higher the loss in productivity.

KMIM effectiveness factor

The KMIM effectiveness factor can be determined by combining the results obtained from monitoring the four different components, namely intellectual capital, financial capital, performance and knowledge-sharing activities, and knowledge gap assessment. There is a direct relationship between the KMIM effectiveness factor and both intellectual and financial capital. There is also a direct relationship between the KMIM effectiveness factor and overall staff performance, including knowledge-sharing activities. This means that the increased participation of staff in knowledge-sharing activities such as communities of practice, discussion forums, focus groups, teamwork and informal networks will impact positively on the overall performance of the organization.

There is also an inverse relationship between the KMIM effectiveness factor and knowledge gaps. The effectiveness factor will increase if the knowledge gaps within the organization can be minimized. After all, one of the main objectives of any knowledge management exercise is to be able to identify knowledge gaps and try to deal with them. The existence of knowledge gaps within the organization has a negative impact on the financial and intellectual capital as well as the overall performance of the organization. Given the above relationships, a formula can be derived to evaluate the KMIM effectiveness factor (E):

$$E = \frac{(P + KS + IC + FC)}{KG}$$

where E is the KMIM effectiveness measure; P is performance at the individual and the group level; KS is the knowledge-sharing activities at the individual and the group level; IC is the intellectual capital; FC is the financial capital; and KG is the knowledge gaps.

4

The role of technology in knowledge management

Introduction

Technology plays an important role in knowledge management, although knowledge management is not about technology. The advances in information and communication technologies, the Internet revolution and the move toward the information and knowledge society have highlighted the importance of knowledge and the need for knowledge management. Information technology has improved our ability to store, access, manipulate, and use information in varieties of ways. It provides us with the ability to improve communications between people and stimulate collaboration. While technology cannot mandate human collaboration, if used effectively it will streamline work operations and improve communications between people. Collaborative applications such as e-mail, calendaring, scheduling, shared folders/databases, and threaded discussions promote knowledge sharing and knowledge transfer.

Many researchers and practitioners attempt to make a distinction between technologies for knowledge management and technologies for information management. According to Duffy (2001), information management primarily focuses on finding work-related objects and moving them around while knowledge management concerns itself with finding and moving work objects as well as with how they are created and used. One other key distinction is that the means of creating, capturing, and communicating in knowledge management systems is very broad, while the focus in information management tools tends to be on electronic transmission of information. Information management is only one component in knowledge management given that knowledge management involves many of the human factors associated with knowledge. To support the various activities of knowledge (explicit knowledge, 'know-how,' 'know-who,' and tacit knowledge), knowledge management tools need to go beyond information management activities and focus on tools that will enable human communications and collaboration.

Amrit (2000) illustrated the difference between knowledge management systems and information management tools using the concept of a data warehouse as an example. According to Amrit, a knowledge management system supports both formal and informal (highly unstructured as well as highly structured) content. It supports informal content such as video content, audio recordings, scribbles, conversations, doodles on notepads, etc. A data warehouse focuses more on highly structured content and does not support informal content. A knowledge management system depends more on context rather than on data or information. The content focus of a knowledge management system is on highly filtered information and on knowledge derived from this information. It requires more complex types of information retrieval and classification tools and therefore the performance requirements are more demanding than those needed for information processing such as with a database management system or in data warehousing applications.

In reality, most knowledge management projects undertaken by organizations are a mix of knowledge consultancy types of work and information management. De Long, Davenport, and Beers (1997) identified a number of characteristics that differentiate knowledge management projects from traditional information management projects. One of the important characteristics is that the goals of knowledge management projects put more emphasis on the value-added for users and not simply on the delivery and accessibility of information. Knowledge management projects support organizational improvement and innovation and not just existing operations; they add value to content by filtering, synthesizing, interpreting, and pruning content and usually require ongoing user contributions and feedback, not just a one-way transfer of information.

Technology-enabling roles

Knowledge management technologies overlap the enabling roles in knowledge management and many of the technology tools can be used to support different knowledge management activities. It is difficult to classify or categorize technology tools according to functionality or even the enabling role, but rather easier to discuss the various technologies on their own. In this section we will discuss some of the knowledge management activities and the roles technology plays in supporting these activities.

Knowledge creation

Knowledge creation is a knowledge management activity that refers to the discovery and generation of new knowledge. Knowledge can be generated through various means including experimentation, observation, training, interaction with the environment, research, and innovative thinking. Some of the knowledge created is codified or documented as explicit knowledge. The rest of the knowledge generated resides in people's minds as tacit knowledge in the form of skills and competencies. Technology plays an important role in facilitating the knowledge-creation process. It provides us with the necessary tools that enable experimentation to take place, and that enable us to record and analyse the results of that experimentation and subsequently to translate those results into products and services. Some of these technologies include mind-mapping tools, simulations, collaborative writing tools, data and text mining, visualization tools and so on.

Knowledge capture

Knowledge capture is a knowledge management activity that enables the organization to identify knowledge sources and to try to capture that knowledge or assist in transferring it from one person to another. Knowledge in the form of 'know-how' can be captured and codified and most organizations would like to retain this knowledge. The organizational knowledge resources in the form of the 'know-how' vary from one organization to another, examples including competitor intelligence, customer information, internal products and service information and so on. Knowledge capture describes the process by which the 'know-how' and 'know-who' can be documented and stored.

The benefits of codifying or capturing 'know-how' knowledge are numerous. The capturing process is a difficult task, but when executed successfully, it will ensure the retention of knowledge in the organization. Technology facilitates knowledge capture through various tools such as document imaging, optical character recognition, data warehousing, e-learning tools, e-mail, and customer relations management tools. 'Ask the expert' tools can also be used to capture questions and answers and make them available to the rest of the people in the organization.

Knowledge sharing and transfer

Knowledge sharing is a very important activity in knowledge management. Today's information technology has provided us with a number of solutions that can cut the down time and budget for knowledge sharing. Nevertheless the most important aspect of knowledge sharing is the human factor. People and culture hold the keys for any successful knowledge-sharing activity. Technology plays the role of enabler by facilitating the information dissemination process, connecting people and systems and enhancing access to large depositories of information. There are many examples of IT tools that can facilitate the distribution of information and in the process enhance knowledge transfer. E-mail, online discussion forums, video-conferencing, and collaboration tools enable knowledge sharing within the organization. Today, with the use of technology, knowledge sharing is extended beyond the organization as individuals can now quickly and easily access information from anywhere at any time. Such tools also enable the sharing of ideas among the employees in the organization and facilitate user participation in decision-making processes. According to Lee and Hong (2002), these tools can help organizations improve learning, sharing, and cooperation among all levels of employees and even with external customers or suppliers.

Knowledge retention

Most organizations realize the importance of knowledge retention, either in the form of explicit knowledge (information) or in the form of tacit knowledge or human and customer capital. In either case, knowledge retention is a difficult task that requires a system and process. Technology facilitates the storage and organization of information. Some of the tools that can be used for knowledge retention include database management systems, text retrieval systems, document management systems, data warehousing, intranets, and so on. Technology also facilitates the storage and retrieval of such information. Knowledge organization tools such as metadata, taxonomies, and ontology are very important if knowledge retention is to be effective.

Leveraging knowledge

The identification and capture of knowledge should lead to knowledge utilization and use. It does not make sense for an organization to spend money and time on knowledge capture unless this knowledge is going to be used effectively in the creation of new products and services. Knowledge that has been captured, stored, retrieved, and analyzed should be leveraged for strategic and tactical decision-making and problem-solving. Upon accessing, understanding, and conceptualizing the knowledge available via the process of knowledge sharing, new knowledge is created. Technology can assist in making knowledge ready for the decision-making process. Some of the tools that can be used to leverage knowledge include visualization tools, data analysis and reporting tools, decision support systems, data and text mining tools, and so on.

Figure 4.1 shows the five differrent dimensions of knowledge management activities discussed above in which technology plays an important role.

Knowledge management enabling tools

As we discussed earlier, one important component of knowledge management is information management. Information management tools are concerned with the management of explicit knowledge or information and include tools for capturing, indexing, retrieving, and manipulating information, for example as database management systems, data warehousing, document management systems, data mining, and so on. Knowledge management technologies go beyond information management

Figure 4.1 The five dimensions of knowledge management activities

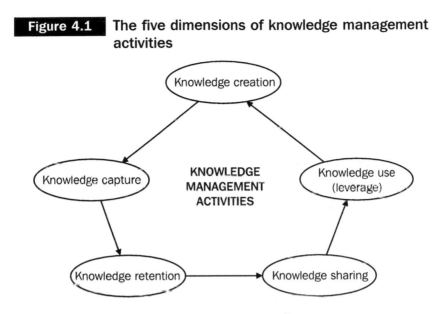

tools to include technologies designed to facilitate the management of other types of knowledge such as tacit knowledge, 'know-how,' and 'know-who.' These technologies require human interaction at all levels and the main objective is to facilitate communication, collaboration, and interaction that in return will facilitate knowledge transfer from one person to another.

The Internet is probably one of the most significant enabling technologies in knowledge management. The Internet today is considered one of the biggest depositories of information ever to exist – it is a platform for communication and collaboration between people around the world. It is also a platform for launching other knowledge management enabling tools such as e-learning tools, web-based collaboration tools, information and knowledge portals, intranets, extranets and, most importantly, a gateway to many resources around the globe. Intranets and extranets provide a gateway to organization knowledge depositories. Besides acting as a platform for the distribution of information and publications, intranets provide the backbone platform for push technology to deliver information to users' desktops. Figure 4.2 shows the four different types of knowledge and the different types of knowledge management tools that can be used to manage or facilitate knowledge transfer.

Knowledge portals

A knowledge portal is an integrated set of knowledge management enabling tools and technologies. Today it is one of the fastest growing areas in knowledge management as far as technology is concerned. A portal can be described as a gateway or a one-stop access to products and information sources over the Web, while knowledge portals can be described as applications that enable companies to unlock internally and externally stored information and provide users with a single gateway to personalized information needed to make informed business decisions. Figure 4.3 shows the evolution of knowledge portals. The advances in the Internet, e-commerce, and information portals have contributed significantly to the evolution of knowledge portals. Many corporate intranets have started to evolve into knowledge portals by incorporating facilities such as collaboration tools, discussion forums, advance search and extraction facilities and, most importantly, personalization whereby users are able to customize interfaces and control information broadcasted to them.

One of the key technologies used in knowledge portals is document management which plays an important role in knowledge retention and knowledge organization. A primary function of any document management system is to allow the effective and efficient handling of large amounts of documents that originate from a variety of sources. Organizations produce and circulate large amounts of information each day, and

Figure 4.2 Knowledge management technologies

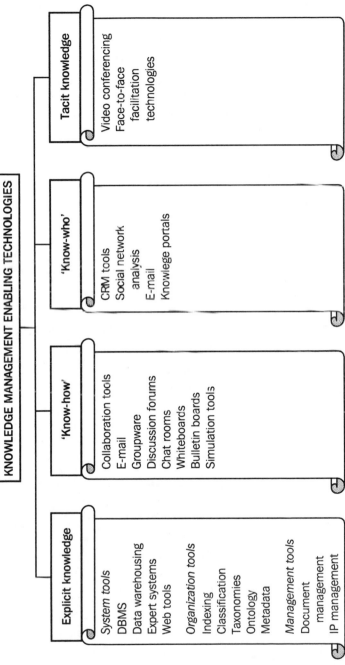

KNOWLEDGE MANAGEMENT ENABLING TECHNOLOGIES

Explicit knowledge

System tools
DBMS
Data warehousing
Expert systems
Web tools

Organization tools
Indexing
Classification
Taxonomies
Ontology
Metadata

Management tools
Document
  management
IP management

'Know-how'

Collaboration tools
E-mail
Groupware
Discussion forums
Chat rooms
Whiteboards
Bulletin boards
Simulation tools

'Know-who'

CRM tools
Social network
  analysis
E-mail
Knowlege portals

Tacit knowledge

Video conferencing
Face-to-face
  facilitation
  technologies

Figure 4.3 Knowledge portal evolution

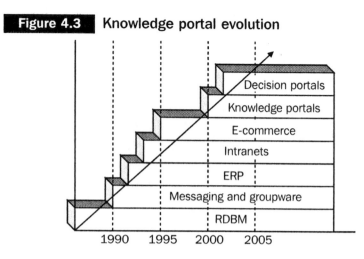

document management systems are used to capture, store and make this information searchable and available to users over the network.

Document management systems involve the integration of different software packages such as imaging tools, optical character recognition tools, database management systems, text retrieval, workflow management, document presentation and reporting tools. Some of the functions supported by document management systems include the following.

Document capturing and indexing

Document capturing tools include the scanning of paper documents, converting images to text using optical character recognition tools, and categorization and indexing tools. Scanning a document produces a raster image that can be stored and indexed in the database. Advances in scanning technology make paper document conversion fast, inexpensive, and easy.

Document capture also involves the capture of documents created in electronic formats such as office suite documents, graphics, audio clips or video files, and storage in a document imaging system. Files can be 'dragged and dropped' into an imaging system but are modifiable and remain in their native format. These files can be viewed in their original format by either launching the original application or by using an embedded file viewer from within the imaging system. Most of these features are now web-based and can be viewed using Internet browsers.

Storage and retrieval

The core of the document management system is the database and the search engines supporting the storage and retrieval of documents. The choice of storage devices is driven by several factors: first, frequency of use, and second, the speed of access required. Storage space used to be of great concern in the early 1990s when document-imaging systems were first introduced. Today, with the advances in storage media such as optical disks and CD-Rom, the storage of large numbers of scanned images is no longer a problem. What is more important today is the indexing and organization of large amounts of information for effective and efficient retrieval.

With optical character recognition (OCR) and pattern matching, the text of scanned images can be converted, indexed, and made accessible. Searching for relevant information as and when you need it is the real challenge. Document management systems can improve document retrieval through the use of metadata, taxonomies and knowledge-mapping techniques.

Workflow management

Workflow is an important component of document management. It allows the organization to have better control over the movement of documents within the organization. Workflow is defined as the coordination of tasks, data and people to make a business process more efficient, effective and adaptable to change. It supports functions such as authoring, revising, routing, commenting, approval, modifications, and conditional branching, and the establishment of deadlines and milestones.

Workflow management systems can also be used to monitor the movement of documents from one user to another, to collect statistics, to assign security rights at different levels, and to generate various types of reports.

The difference between a workflow and an e-mail system is in the level of security and control which a workflow provides. Portal security is critical to the operations which take place within the organization. A document imaging system should provide security at multiple levels, including security at the level of individual documents within the database.

The characteristics of a knowledge portal

The key features and characteristics of a knowledge portal vary from one organization to another, depending on the functionality of the portal and the types of application deployed on the web server. Figure 4.4 shows the structure of a knowledge portal along with some of the technologies and tools that can be integrated into the portal. In this section we discuss some of these characteristics and their importance in knowledge management.

Personalization

Personalization of content enables users to create their own personal workplace according to a set of preferences that enables them to view the content they are interested in while having all irrelevant information automatically filtered out. A knowledge portal should also allow information to dynamically deliver

Figure 4.4 Knowledge portal structure

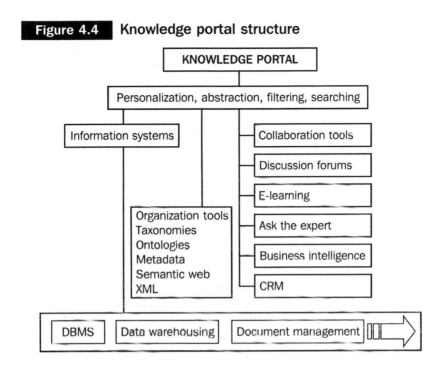

specific content to users. For example, the Hummingbird enterprise knowledge portal (EKP) incorporates a variety of unique features that allows users to create their very own web-based workspace. Users can build multi-page environments to customize the portal to their individual needs and provide for maximum productivity gain (Watson and Fenner, 2000). Moreover, users can develop and choose from various themes that provide a personal or corporate look and feel, as well as the ability to apply platform-specific interfaces for desktop PCs and palm devices.

Information-gathering and capture through application integration

The ability to extract and index information from disparate sources such as file servers, databases, business systems, groupware systems, document repositories, legacy systems, and the Web is a key feature of a knowledge portal. Information-gathering can be conducted by both proactive and reactive methods such as user- or administrator-initiated searches, web crawling, site and directory monitoring, full-text indexing, and indexing of metadata and taxonomies. Hyperwave eKnowledge Suite, for example, accepts a wide range of document formats from a variety of authoring tools so that users can stick with the tools they know such as Microsoft Windows and Microsoft Office (Kappe, 2001). Products such as Plumtree and Hummingbird provide users with a centralized, unified and consistent environment for interactions with all applications and hence information-gathering by simplifying the process of building the portal and incorporating the various KM components that the business requires.

Automatic and manual classification and organization of information

Besides providing automatic indexing, a knowledge portal should support taxonomy-building and knowledge-mapping facilities. Such tools will help in organizing information according to hierarchies or categorization that facilitate navigation and easy access to information. Grouping related pieces of information together into some classification scheme or taxonomy facilitates information retrieval in large databases. Due to the cost of organizing information manually, an automatic categorization or semi-automatic categorization can be used in which the system can be 'trained' using, for example, neural networks.

Some portals also allow hyperlink management that is automatic since hyperlinks relate pieces of information to each other in context and thus represent an important part of managing knowledge. Automatic summary is also another organizing feature in which a short text representation of a document is produced by extracting the most relevant sentences. This would be useful in assessing the value of a set of documents, in particular in situations where the user is on low bandwidth or using a small-screen device such as a PDA or mobile phone.

Search/navigation

Good searching and navigation tools mean better access to knowledge sources within the organization. A knowledge portal normally provides basic and advanced-searching options including Boolean, free-text, proximity, and fielded searches. Within the free-text search, users should be able to use more advanced features such as a thesaurus, stemming, phonetic, fuzzy logic, similarity, and XML or metadata searches. Browsing and navigation, on the other hand, are knowledge work activities that go hand in hand with the search function (Mack et al., 2001). Browsing and navigation should be intuitive and supported by a user-friendly interface and instinctive classification/taxonomy schemes.

Distribution and publishing

The knowledge portal is a good platform for information publishing and distribution. As knowledge portals are used as a single point of entry in the organization, information published on the portal is more feasible and reaches a wider audience. Knowledge delivery could take the form of web distribution, web content management, push delivery via agents and subscriptions, and e-mail notifications.

Locating expertise ('ask the expert')

Many of the knowledge portals provide contact management and 'ask the expert' facilities. This allows users to post questions to the expert listed on the website. The expert can be internal or external. When the expert answers the question, a copy of the question and the answer are captured in the database. The next time another user asks the same question, the system is able to retrieve the answer and make it available to the user. Besides locating experts, it is also as important for the knowledge portal to allow individuals to declare their expertise in a given area and for the portal to infer an individual's expertise based on actions such as courses completed under an e-learning environment. These two methods of determining expertise would help keep the expertise database current and updated.

Access control

Security is a primary concern for all organizations. As knowledge portals are intended as gateways or windows to the organization's resources, there is a need to provide different levels of security depending on the type of users and the type of material accessed. As an example, Hummingbird developed a technology called the Common Authentication Protocol (CAP) server that delivers a single login model to Hummingbird portals. By entering a single password and username, users gain access to all data sources, applications, and collaborative tools they would normally have in a client/server network environment. From an administrative standpoint, user authentication is managed through existing security profiles (such as LDAP – Lightweight Directory Access Protocol, an Internet protocol), eliminating the need to create and maintain additional security accounts for users. Built-in encryption and support for standard authentication models minimize required security maintenance (Messmer and Mears, 2002).

Information extraction and analysis

Knowledge portals provide for information extraction and filtering using tools such as business intelligence, expert systems, and statistical analysis. The emphasis on content and value-added services is one of the features that distinguish knowledge portals from information portals. Some people refer to knowledge portals that focus on context and data analysis as decision portals. This is because information extracted from the knowledge store and other disparate data sources to conduct data analysis and mining can help executives in the organization in the decision-making process.

Collaboration

One of the key features that distinguish knowledge portals from information portals is the collaboration and activities that take place on the web server. Knowledge portals provide a platform for people to engage in discussion and exchange information. This framework includes interactive facilities such as chat sessions, bulletin boards, and application sharing together with shared workspaces, whiteboards, and collaboration and authoring tools. Collaboration is also aided by business process automation capabilities such as routing and workflow.

Collaborative technologies are often seen as the platform that brings people together to share expertise, irrespective of time, location, and space constraints. The objectives here are to achieve business goals and improve organizational learning and innovation. It is also believed that collaboration assists in the process of capturing tacit knowledge, although problems still exist in translating the tacit knowledge captured into explicit knowledge. The following is a brief summary of some of the common collaboration tools used in knowledge portals.

E-mail and messaging systems

E-mail is one of the most popular and powerful collaborative applications. Messaging technology allows people to communicate at any time and anywhere at a very low cost. Today, messaging systems using mobile devices are among the most widely used wireless applications. The key concept in an e-mail system is that neither the senders nor the recipients are connected to each other in any way other than via their respective e-mail servers. Hence, in the context of collaboration, the e-mail allows people to communicate and interact without having to be present in a specified location.

Groupware applications

Groupware applications support and encourage joint workgroup activities. Groupware applications are diverse in function but most include a shared database and folders where team members can work on common documents and hold electronic discussions (Miller and Slater, 2000). Some include group schedulers, calendaring, and e-mail. In addition, others may focus on real-time meeting support. Together, these features allow team members to work on a single document, discuss ideas online, maintain records, and prioritize and schedule teamwork and meetings. A genuine groupware package should include several of these functions, not just one. Two of the most popular groupware applications are Lotus Notes and Microsoft Exchange.

Discussion groups, forums, and bulletin boards

Discussion boards and groups allow individuals to send messages to each other and the messages get posted to the subscribers of the same discussion list. People on the same list can respond to the posting and so a discussion commences, allowing a debate to take place. Bulletin boards also share the same concept in which users can post and read messages posted by others to the discussion thread. Software tools are available to help organise the threads of conversations that may be occurring simultaneously.

The purpose of forums is to create a public dialogue and deliberation on issues which would not be possible otherwise due to geographical constraints. The intent here is to increase the participants' understanding of various perspectives on an issue through dialogue focusing on values and experiences that underlie opinions.

Online chat

Online chat is a tool that provides synchronous text-based communication between two computers. Synchronous here means that there are at least two people on two different computers communicating with each in real time. Typically, users will be connected to a chat server using a chat client and meet in a chat room. Once the users are in the same chat room, they can converse with one another by typing messages into a window where all of the other users in the chat room can see the messages. The user can also see all of the messages entered by the other users.

Audio and video/desktop conferencing

Advanced and integrated audio and video conferencing technology supports concepts such as virtual teams, communities of practice, telecommuting, and remote conferencing, which aid collaboration between knowledge workers. Desktop conferencing connects a group of users, for example to share ideas, exchange information, carry out discussions, or deliver course material in virtual classroom settings. Audio and video conferencing allows for better communication among workers as context and body language are better interpreted. This is especially useful in the transfer of tacit knowledge.

Whiteboards

The whiteboard tools allow groups of users to share a common graphical palette synchronously. An object appears on the whiteboard of all users once a user draws something and releases their mouse button. All connected users can modify this same object at that point in time. Functions include the ability to insert text and graphics, choose fonts and colors, fill and unfill objects, move objects and modify them. The whiteboard is also sometimes labelled a brainstorming tool that helps inspire creative thinking and convert tacit understanding into explicit knowledge.

5

Knowledge sharing

Introduction

Today, large amounts of information are being shared freely over the Internet and through subscriptions to databases and information repositories. Knowledge sharing, in its broadest sense, refers to the communication of all types of knowledge, which includes explicit knowledge or information, the 'know-how' and 'know-who' which are types of knowledge that can be documented and captured as information, and tacit knowledge in the form of skills and competencies. Tacit knowledge is personal and can only be shared through socialization, interaction, and training. It requires face-to-face communication and in most cases it gets transferred through observation, imitation, practice, and interaction with the environment. Effective sharing involves the actions of transmission and absorption by the sender and potential receiver respectively. If knowledge is received but not absorbed, as in the case of information transfer, then the knowledge transfer process is not considered complete. For knowledge transfer to take place, it has to be received, processed, and absorbed (Davenport and Prusak, 1998). The critical outcome of knowledge sharing is the creation of new knowledge and innovation that will significantly improve organizational performance. O'Dell and Grayson (1998) believe that for knowledge sharing to work, organizations must embrace the internal transfer of knowledge as a core process designed to deliver dramatic and sustainable improvement in performance.

Many terms have been used for knowledge sharing, among them knowledge transfer, dissemination, exchange, and distribution. Defining knowledge sharing as the deliberate act in which knowledge is made reusable for one party through its transfer by another places more emphasis on the knowledge transfer process. The transfer typically transcends geographical distance and time. It may be unidirectional or bidirectional, it may be vertical (between superior and subordinate) or horizontal (between peers). Knowledge sharing also takes place outside the organization – with customers, suppliers, strategic alliance partners, collaborators, regulators, etc. The knowledge transfer can take many forms. It can be in the form of writing books or research papers. Natarajan and Shekhar (2000) stated that the irresistible urge to share knowledge propelled them to write their book. Knowledge transfer can occur while delivering a lecture or making a speech or presentation. One example is the US President's State of the Union Address. The US Constitution requires the president to update (read as 'share knowledge with') the Congress on the State of the Union. Many countries have their own 'State of the Nation Address' delivered by their heads of state for the same purpose.

Participating in a dialogue over coffee or lunch is another form of knowledge and information sharing. For example, when Xerox's technical representatives – repairmen – swap 'war stories' about malfunctioning copiers that outstripped the documentation and classroom instruction, in the process of telling and analysing such stories the reps both feed into and draw on the group's collective knowledge. Storytelling is useful in preserving the organizational memory, and can be used to convey values, build *esprit de corps*, create role models, reveal how things work around the organization, and communicate complex ideas (Stewart, 1998). Participating in communities of practice (COPs), which are informal, ad hoc, spontaneous groups of people who voluntarily share similar interests and goals, is yet another avenue for knowledge sharing. COPs enable an organization to tap into knowledge that is generated and held collectively.

Collaborating in a research effort culminating in the writing of a joint paper necessarily requires knowledge sharing to work. Price (1963) reported that such collaborative work had been increasing steadily and ever more rapidly since the beginning of the twentieth century, as indicated by the proportion of multi-author papers which was growing steadily. He also noted that in physics, collaborative work exceeded single-author papers (Price, 1961).

As knowledge represents power, knowledge sharing is an unnatural act in most organizations. With the recognition that knowledge is a valuable resource, this may make the situation worse as making knowledge public may be seen as threatening. What is natural is knowledge hoarding. The 'not invented here' syndrome also predominates. Hence, compensation and performance evaluation must be used to encourage knowledge sharing and knowledge reuse.

The need for knowledge sharing

The question is, why share knowledge? There are several reasons that make this activity essential. Many industrial countries today are faced with an ageing population, implying a graying workforce for many organizations. This has led to the requirement that the knowledge that they have accumulated over the years be codified in some form and 'passed on' before they retire. In the US, the older population – persons 65 years or older – numbered 34.5 million in 1999. They represented 12.7 percent of the US population, about one in every eight Americans (FIFARS, 2000). In Singapore, this figure is 7.3 percent (Leow,

2000). The immense pool of experience possessed by this cohort has to be passed to the next generation of workers. Other than through retirement, knowledge can be lost through redundancy, resignation and even through promotion.

Drucker (1994) proposes that applied knowledge is only effective when highly specialized. Highly specialized knowledge workers mean that teams become the work unit rather than the individual himself. They become productive only if combined together into a single, unified knowledge. This can be seen in the 97-hour operation to separate the conjoined twins Ganga and Jamuna that took place in Singapore where a multidisciplinary team of specialists comprising neurosurgeons, plastic surgeons, anesthetists, pediatricians, neurologists, a geneticist, a dietician, and physical, speech and occupational therapists participated. In fact, Dr Chumpon Chan and Dr Keith Goh, the neurosurgeons who led the team, attributed the success of the surgery and the fact that the team was able to sustain the lengthy procedure to great teamwork – having an implicit trust in each other, being able to hand over part of what one is doing, having a rest and knowing that one's fellow surgeon is going to carry on and do a good job (SingHealth, 2000).

Today, organizations have an enormous amount of knowledge assets. As an example (and this example considers only one type of explicit knowledge), Lucent and its predecessor companies have been issued with more than 37,000 patents dating back to the 1800s. They currently obtain patents at a rate of three per day. Much knowledge sharing has to take place to take advantage of the knowledge silos that exist in organizations – to avoid reinventing the wheel, to reduce duplication and replication of effort, and to avoid the same errors. When Intel embarked on an effort to accelerate the development process of microprocessors, they found that 'more than 60 percent of the problems [they] faced had been encountered and solved earlier by another team' (Yu, 1998: 194).

A highly mobile workforce with frequent global travel supported through technologies like hot-desking (or hotelling), where workers do not have their own desks but share the available workspace depending on their needs, is a common practice in organizations in which staff spend a lot of time out of the office meeting clients. There has been an increase in the number of large, distributed organizations, in part brought about by the number of mega-mergers. For example, the Exxon Mobil Corporation, ranked number 1 in both Fortune 500 and Global 500 in 2001, has 123,000 employees worldwide and supplies refined petrochemical products to more than 40,000 service stations in 118 countries that operate under the Exxon, Esso and Mobil brands. This has in turn led to an increase in virtual teams – teams that work across distance, time zones, and organizational boundaries, and whose members may never meet at all except in cyberspace. 'Working together apart' presents its own set of problems. Besides the time difference, team members are deprived of each other's non-verbal communication cues – facial expressions, gestures and vocal inflections which provide clues to their colleagues' opinions, attitudes, and emotions.

Deciphering the meaning of text-based messages like the e mail can sometimes be confusing, especially when the writer/sender is trying to be sarcastic or facetious (Gould, 1997). Getting together for lunch is impossible, and so is dropping by informally in each other's offices. These large organizations have a large portfolio of products and services, far too many for any one person to comprehend, but the same idea can be adapted to different processes, products, or services.

Competition is based on speed to market and shortening product life-cycles. Intel accelerated the development process for microprocessors and ensured the quick harvesting of research results by collocating the process development and production groups to facilitate the exchange of ideas and to enable the groups to gain an understanding of the issues they faced (Yu, 1998).

One of the difficulties in getting people to share knowledge emanates from the nature of knowledge itself. Knowledge is personal, mobile, and portable, and knows no boundaries. This has made knowledge sharing potentially dangerous, in that a good idea can be easily copied once it has been shared. In the 1970s, the idea of the graphical user interface (GUI) was developed at the Xerox Palo Alto Research Center (PARC). Steve Jobs, one of the co-founders of Apple, was invited to tour the research facility and was immediately struck by the possibilities of GUI. He went back to Apple determined that the next generation of machines they would market would have the same style of user interface as the one they had seen at PARC (Edwards, 1995).

Knowledge-sharing models

Several models and frameworks were proposed for knowledge sharing. Such models and frameworks can be used to articulate and understand the different factors that impact knowledge sharing in an organization. They also provide the basis for an assessment of the current practices of knowledge sharing and help map the desired state in the future. In this section we discuss some of these models and frameworks.

The actors framework

The actors framework proposed by Lee and Al-Hawamdeh (2002) views knowledge sharing as a process taking place between two actors (see Figure 5.1). This might take place between two people in a one-to-one relationship such as a conversation over a cup of coffee, in a one-to-many relationship such as a person giving a presentation or delivering a speech, in a many-to-one relationship such as in a group of authors 'speaking' to a person through their co-written book, or in a many-to-many relationship such as in a

Figure 5.1 The actors framework

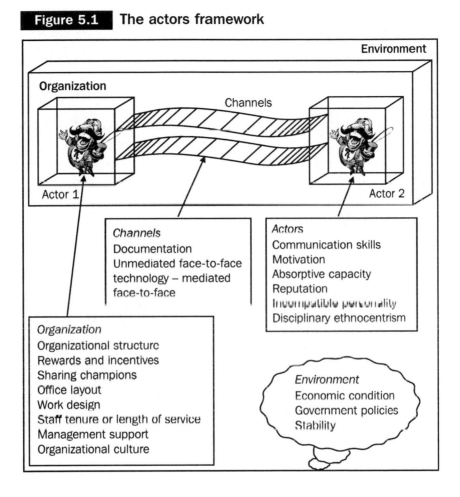

working team presenting to the judges. The process uses one of three channels:

- face-to-face: unmediated (as in a telephone conversation);
- face-to-face: technology mediated (as in video conferencing);
- through a document (as in a videotaped recording of a cooking demonstration).

Factors affecting knowledge sharing can arise from the actors, the knowledge being shared, the channel, the organization, or the broader environmental climate.

Factors arising from the actors

These factors arise because of an attribute belonging to one or both of the actors in the knowledge-sharing process. A modification of these factors will require a modification of the attributes of the actors. The mobility of knowledge workers, resulting in teams where members originate from different countries and speak different first languages, makes this problem worse.

The factors include:

- communication skills
- people skills
- motivation
- absorptive capacity
- reputation
- appreciation of the importance of knowledge
- incompatible personality
- disciplinary ethnocentrism
- technophobia.

Factors arising from the channel

The channel is the medium by which knowledge is communicated or passed from one party to another. A major difference with the three channels is the richness of the communication that is possible. The printed document is not able to convey rich, tacit knowledge. Face-to-face mediated by technology is better; for example, video conferencing enables passion and enthusiasm, facial expressions and voice inflections to be conveyed. Face-to-face unmediated has the largest bandwidth.

The factors include:

- documentation
- face-to-face unmediated
- face-to-face technology mediated.

Factors arising from the organizational environment

The organizational environment in which the knowledge-sharing process takes place imposes its own set of barriers:

- organizational structure
- reward system and incentives for knowledge sharing
- availability of knowledge-sharing champions
- office layout
- work design
- staff tenure or length of service
- management support
- organizational culture.

An environment of trust is conducive to knowledge sharing. Intel practises constructive confrontation, where employees are 'encouraged to say when they disagree with someone else's idea or proposal, whether it comes from a peer, subordinate, or a boss' (Yu, 1998: 112). This practice is considered essential to enable senior management to hear all points before they make decisions. Trust is clearly a prerequisite for this practice.

The way in which decisions are made is also important. Companies adopting autocratic styles, where decisions are made by edict, are less likely to succeed in knowledge sharing compared to organizations where participatory or consensual decision-making styles are employed. The attitude of workers under strict, top-down management would probably be 'why bother?'

Factors arising from the characteristics of the knowledge being shared

Some knowledge is easier to share than others. Levitt (1989) describes the ability of Babe Ruth to hit home runs as such a form of knowledge. While he couldn't explain it, it didn't prevent him from hitting homers. The possessor of the knowledge does not need to know what he knows in order to use it. Nonaka (1991) describes the bread-making process as another such example and calls this form of knowledge tacit knowledge, deeply embedded into an organization's operating practices. Knowledge that does not have a proven track record will also be harder to sell.

Factors arising from the climate

These are barriers arising from 'the larger picture.' Three examples are the economic condition of the nation, governmental policies, and societal culture. Bonaventura (1997) has suggested that when jobs are at stake, networks are withdrawn and individual knowledge is closely guarded as protection against termination. Such a scenario may occur when the nation is experiencing an economic downturn. Government policies such as the Foreign Talent Policy in Singapore (aimed at attracting foreign talent and skilled workers), if not well justified to the people, may create dissatisfaction and breed resentment, creating barriers to the sharing of knowledge either way – foreign talent to local and vice versa.

Societal culture also impacts knowledge sharing. East Asian societies (e.g. China, Japan, Taiwan, and Singapore), are strongly influenced by Confucianism, the characteristics of which are the tight organization of society, stratified interaction (communication which is dependent on the rank or gender of the actors), a collectivist pressure (pressure to conform and win approval), an emphasis on order and harmony, an avoidance of conflict, hierarchies (respect for the senior members of the organization), and a tendency for self-criticism (modesty when appraising themselves). It may be more difficult for a member in such a society to share knowledge. On the other hand, Western societies (e.g. America, Britain, Canada, Australia, and New Zealand), which are strongly influenced by liberal individualism, tend to be loosely organized, individualistic (an emphasis on the uniqueness of the individual), and egalitarian (less emphasis on rank and status), with a tendency for self-enhancement (more likely to regard themselves in a positive light) (Ng, 2001). Although this may create the ideal environment for knowledge sharing, it can also work in the opposite direction. Teamwork may be difficult to achieve, and an argument or point of view may be carried on for longer than is productive.

Model for best practice transfer from O'Dell and Grayson

O'Dell and Grayson (1998) proposed a model for best-practice transfer to create a successful knowledge-sharing environment in an organization (see Figure 5.2). Their model has three major components, namely three value propositions (objectives and reasons for managing knowledge), four enablers (conducive environment to share knowledge), and a four-step change process (structured process to implement initiatives). The model presents an enabling environment that will support the whole activity in achieving the value proposition. The value proposition differs from one organization to another as each organization will select the value that is most beneficial and practical.

The enabling environment consists of four components. The first component is culture. Culture varies from one organization to another. Knowledge sharing and knowledge transfer should

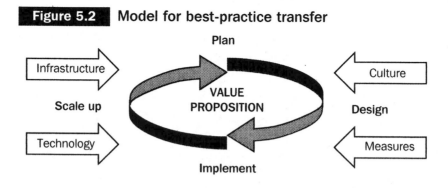

Figure 5.2 Model for best-practice transfer

take into account the culture within the organization. The second component is measurement. It is very difficult to measure intellectual capacity and intangible assets. However, organizations can set up their own measurements to assess the level of achievements. The third component is infrastructure. This refers to the organizational structure, networks, knowledge resources, processes, and so on. The fourth component is technology. This involves advances in technology and their importance to the knowledge-sharing environment. Such technologies include data communication and networking, collaboration tools and other communication infrastructure. Communication within the organization or among organizations can be carried out in a faster and more reliable manner.

Inkpen and Dinur's knowledge transfer model

This model was proposed in a working paper in 1998 by Inkpen and Dinur and used the term knowledge spectrum as a core concept. The knowledge spectrum as discussed in the paper consists of the total knowledge an organization may be able to utilize. The knowledge spectrum is shaped and defined by five contextual dimensions, namely: culture, strategy, decision-making, environment, and technology and operations. Each of these dimensions contributes to the knowledge spectrum's shape and size. The knowledge contextual dimensions and central variables as outlined in the working paper are:

1. Culture:
   - Fit between culture and knowledge
   - Culture clash and differences among units
   - Organizational and national cultures

2. Strategy:
   - Choice of strategy
   - Stated goals and objectives
   - Strategic group or niche

3. Decision-making structure and processes:
   - Formal hierarchy
   - Power structure
   - Communication and leadership styles
   - Teamwork, formality, and incentive systems

4. Environment:
   - Uncertainty, and casual ambiguity
   - Industry volatility and life-cycle
   - Location
   - Relationship with other firms as well as with political and legal agents

5. Technology and operations:
   - Education and skills of employees
   - Available physical equipment and experience with similar technology
   - Firm infrastructure
   - Turnover of inventory, equipment, and people
   - Efficiency and quality

The model also identified three types of knowledge pocket that can be transferred within the organization (see Figure 5.3). The first type of knowledge pocket is located within the knowledge spectrum but outside the knowledge state. This type of knowledge has the potential to be turned into competencies provided that it can be discovered, identified, and recognized by the organization. The second type of knowledge pocket is located within the knowledge state and can be turned into competencies as the knowledge is discovered, identified, and recognized. The third type of knowledge pockets exists outside the knowledge spectrum, is incompatible with the organization's knowledge base, and has no potential to become competencies.

Figure 5.3 **Inkpen and Dinur: types of knowledge pocket within the model**

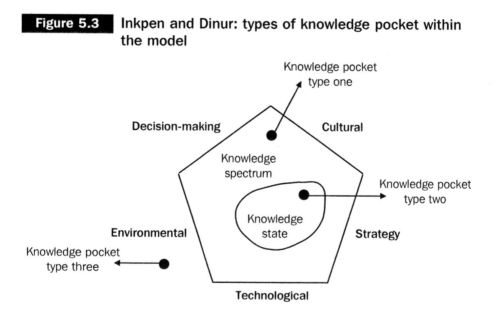

When a knowledge transfer occurs, that means a specific knowledge pocket is being transferred, and it is extracted from the original context and moved to the new context. The contexts themselves were formed by the five dimensions. If two units within the organization face somewhat similar levels of restricting dimensions then their knowledge spectrums will partially overlap. In this case only the knowledge pockets that are located within the overlapping area within the source and the recipient unit's knowledge spectrum can be successfully transferred. Thus, in order for a specific knowledge pocket to be successfully transferred from one organizational unit to another, similar or at least closely related contexts must exist. This means that the closer and more similar of the five dimensions listed above will produce a more successful transfer of knowledge between the organizational units.

Szulanski's knowledge stickiness

Just as a firm's distinctive competencies may be difficult for competitors to imitate, they may be difficult to replicate internally as well. This has resulted in uneven performance from similar units within a company. Szulanski (1996) studied best-practice transfers in eight firms and identified four stages of the transfer process, namely initiation, implementation, ramp-up, and integration:

- *Initiation* comprises all events leading up to the decision to transfer knowledge. A transfer begins when there is a coincidence of a knowledge gap and the knowledge to fill that gap.
- *Implementation* refers to the resource flows between the recipient and source. Social ties are formed and the transferred practice is adapted for use in the recipient unit.
- *Ramp-up* begins when the recipient starts applying the transferred knowledge.
- *Integration* becomes possible once the recipient achieves success with the transferred knowledge. The new practice lose its novelty and becomes routinized and institutionalized in the recipient unit.

He found that the stickiness of knowledge was primarily due to knowledge-related factors like the knowledge recipient's lack of absorptive and retentive capacity, causal ambiguity, and an arduous relationship between the knowledge source and recipient. Motivation-related factors such as a lack of incentives, confidence, and buy-in were found to be of secondary importance.

The SECI model

Nonaka and Takeuchi (1995) proposed the knowledge spiral model (also known as the knowledge creation model – see Figure 5.4) which is concerned with the conversion of tacit knowledge to explicit knowledge and vice versa. They suggested four steps – socialization, externalization, combination, and internalization (SECI) – by which knowledge sharing or knowledge transfer can take place and which highlight the patterns of interaction between tacit and explicit knowledge:

- *Tacit to tacit (socialization).* Tacit knowledge is built through shared experiences, face-to-face meetings, etc. in which the role of information technology is very minimal. However, an increasing proportion of informal meetings and other interpersonal groupware tools can be put in place. Shared experiences are a key attribute for the formation and sharing of tacit knowledge.

- *Tacit to explicit (externalization).* Converting tacit knowledge to explicit knowledge involves and takes place in a shared space and is then articulated through an interactive session. Collaboration systems should play a major part in this type of knowledge transfer. For instance, online newsgroups and forums capture tacit knowledge to apply it to some other external problems.

- *Explicit to explicit (combination).* Once tacit knowledge is articulated it becomes explicit knowledge. Capturing it as a

Figure 5.4 **Knowledge spiral model developed by Nonaka and Takeuchi in 1995**

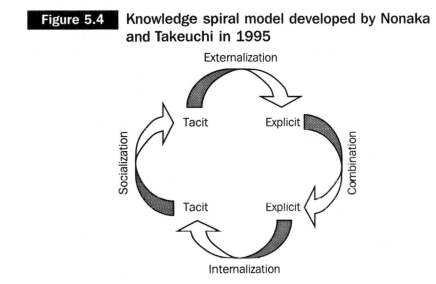

report, an e-mail, a presentation, or a web page makes it available to everyone in the organization. Word processors, document management systems, web documents, etc. can be used for this type of knowledge transfer. Capturing explicit knowledge in this way makes it available to a wider audience.

■ *Explicit to tacit (internalization)*. Generally, better understanding and appreciation of explicit knowledge creates new tacit knowledge. A knowledge management system on top of information retrieval should facilitate the understanding and use of information. Collaborative learning systems play a major part in this type of knowledge transfer.

In the knowledge spiral model, knowledge sharing is a cycle of the four steps discussed above. Knowledge is shared via the different modes depending on the nature of the knowledge and the knowledge context. As proposed by the model, tacit knowledge can be transferred to another person through social contact and interaction. This means that a recipient can pick up tacit knowledge by looking at how experts, or the knowledge source, apply their knowledge.

Cultivating a knowledge-sharing culture

Knowledge sharing is a social activity that can be measured by the level of interaction among people within the organization. Learning and sharing of knowledge first and foremost are social activities and they take place among people. Practices embedded in people, culture, and context are complex. Culture refers to the values and beliefs that people in the organization share. Due to the complexity associated with knowledge sharing, a culture of learning and knowledge sharing needs to be instilled and cultivated within the organization. To inculcate a knowledge-sharing culture, there is a need to change the mindset of the people in the organization and create a climate of trust and openness.

In reality, knowledge sharing is a complex process, especially when someone is trying to change the mindsets, behaviors, and culture of the organization. It is a challenge to identify the factors that actually drive people to share freely what they know. A study by the American Productivity and Quality Center (APQC, 1999: 7–9) identified six key factors that could influence people's willingness to share knowledge:

- knowledge sharing and business strategy;
- the role of human networks;
- the role of leaders and managers;
- fit with the overall culture;
- knowledge sharing and daily work;
- institutionalizing learning disciplines.

The study found that, increasingly, organizations with a collaborative culture often tie their knowledge-sharing initiatives to their business strategies. They share knowledge to solve business problems and achieve specific business results. These companies realize the connection between sharing knowledge and the attainment of business objectives. It is also important to note that recognition and rewards are important factors in influencing individual behaviours and aligning individuals' interests with those of the organization. Human networks are also viewed by best-practice organizations as the key to knowledge sharing. Enabling and supporting informal networks without formalizing them is found to provide a more conducive environment for knowledge-sharing practices. Whether formal or informal, these human networks often have knowledge champions or facilitators who 'own' the network and actively ensure that staff participate. Knowledge professionals can play the role of champions or facilitators in promoting and cultivating a knowledge-sharing culture.

Knowledge professionals can act as a bridge between knowledge workers and management in the organization. Management and leadership are further crucial components in creating a knowledge-sharing culture. The strong influence that the leadership has on the rest of the organization is one of the determining factors. Managers and leaders, together with the knowledge professionals, can help to lead by example and enhance communication and interaction at all levels in the organization.

6

Communication and organizational culture

Introduction

In Chapter 5 we considered the importance of organizational culture in creating and nurturing a knowledge-sharing culture within the organization. Organizational culture is normally reflected in the corporate structure, leadership, management style, norms, and practices. The corporate structure to a large extent affects the communication patterns within the organization and as a result discourages information and knowledge sharing. Leadership looks at how leaders encourage and support the development of a knowledge-conducive environment, how they instill values of sharing in the employees and how they demonstrate their beliefs. Management style examines whether the organization fosters mutual trust between employer and employee and among employees, the level of tolerance for mistakes, and whether the resources (financial, time, and place) are in place for knowledge generation and exchange. Norms and practices reflect the organizational attributes that are essential for KM implementation. They explore the prevalence of continuous learning in the organization, the norms of incorporating knowledge creation into the business process, as well as the practice of rewarding and according recognition to staff.

Cultures have a great influence on the behavior of managers. They can strongly affect the organization's ability to shift its strategic direction and respond to the ever-changing demands of the external environment. Deal and Kennedy (1982) pointed out that a strong culture is a powerful lever in guiding behavior and has a direct impact on employees' morale. Organizational culture forms one of the critical success factors in the implementation of knowledge management within the organization. A healthy culture enhances the prospects of successful implementation of knowledge management. Davenport and Prusak (1998) called cultural factors that inhibit knowledge transfer 'frictions' and proposed ways of overcoming them.

Culture is inherent in most nationalities, groups of individuals, and people of varying demographic segments. It is a product of many years of nurturing, cultivation, and interaction between people on the one hand, and between people and the environment on the other. As culture is deeply rooted, it is not possible to expect organizational culture to be changed easily. Organizational culture and behavior take time to become established and will require a similar amount of time and influence to be changed and altered. Culture is inherently a way of life and the practice of doing things in a certain way or in a certain manner. When an employee moves from one organization to another, their previous practices, behavior, and beliefs might sometimes come into conflict with the existing organizational culture. In certain cases, if the new employee is not able to adjust and adapt to the new culture, he or she might be forced to leave the organization. On the other hand, over time, new employees can influence and change organizational culture. This normally happens faster when new employees are given a bigger managerial role or are recruited to lead the organization. Resistance to change normally occurs when a top-to-bottom approach fails to convince the people in the organization of the need for cultural change.

In multicultural societies, people from different nationalities, races, and cultures with diverse backgrounds and training have come together to live and work. With the globalization of economies and the use of technology to overcome geographical boundaries, organizations are no longer able to shield themselves from the influence of other cultures. When trying to change one's culture in a new organization, conflicts are bound to arise. Norms and practices within the organization can help in dealing with the problem to a certain extent, but the challenge remains when avenues for knowledge sharing and dissemination are explored within an organization where cultural diversity is evident. The implementation of any knowledge management initiative in an organization involves both technical aspects as well as the human factor. The success of any knowledge management practices will depend to a large extent on the successful integration of different skills sets across different cultures with a common goal in mind. Investment in training and teambuilding efforts to foster a strong company identity is one way to achieve success.

Cultural enablers

Organizational culture is normally reflected in the organization's corporate structure, leadership, management style, learning experience, and norms and practices. It influences the perception of the employee about the types of knowledge deemed as important. These parameters significantly contribute to the organization's attributes. In the sections which follow we take a closer look at a number of cultural issues and then consider cultural barriers and their impact on knowledge management practices in the organization (see Figure 6.1).

Figure 6.1 Organizational culture, issues, and barriers

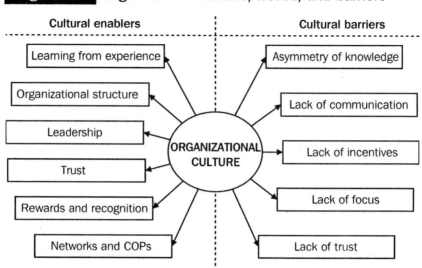

Cultural enablers

Cultural barriers

- Learning from experience
- Organizational structure
- Leadership
- Trust
- Rewards and recognition
- Networks and COPs

ORGANIZATIONAL CULTURE

- Asymmetry of knowledge
- Lack of communication
- Lack of incentives
- Lack of focus
- Lack of trust

Learning from experience

The ability to learn from experience and experimentation is a process that requires continuous adjustments to the norms and practices within the organization. One of the salient features of knowledge management is to cultivate, develop and utilize the learning process to ensure and encourage knowledge sharing and knowledge creation. According to Senge (1990), a learning organization is one where people continually expand their capacity to create the results they truly desire, where new and expansive patterns of thinking are nurtured, where collective aspiration is set free, and where people are continually learning how to learn together.

A willingness to learn and encourage learning is something that has to be rooted in the organizational culture. To find the extent to which the organization culture encourages learning, the following questions may be asked: Does the organization encourage learning? Is formal and informal training part of organizational practice? Does the organization allow learning through experimentation? Is learning through mistakes a norm? Is the organization tolerant of mistakes?

Leonard-Barton (1995) pointed out that the norms of respecting diversity and tolerance of mistakes are essential to the creation of intellectual capital. Learning from mistakes requires courage and a supportive organization structure. Multi-layered management hierarchies most of the time thwart reporting, making it difficult for employees to explain their point of view and avoid repeating the same mistakes.

Organizational structure

Organizational structure plays an important role in shaping organizational culture. It reflects the relationships between people within the organization, the communication pattern, authority, management style, workflow, and the flow of information between people and within different departments. Multi-layered hierarchies or a flat structure say something about the core values that direct the organization's designers and the expectations of its members. Palmer (1998) pointed out that steep functional hierarchies actively promote a culture of distrust and 'not invented here' thinking (see Figure 6.2). Member participation is minimized and discouraged by a hierarchy of approval and red tape. Wenger, McDermott and Snyder (2002) classify this as an anti-learning culture where communities of practice, one of the important elements of knowledge management, are marginalized and their effectiveness reduced. A hierarchical structure normally results in poor coordination across different divisions and hierarchies. This also results in functional inefficiency, conflict, and competition across different product lines and entities within the organization.

Conversely, a matrix structure is less rigid and decision-making is decentralized. Communication channels are more informal, facilitating information flow (see Figure 6.3). Palmer (1998) noted

Figure 6.2 Divisional structure

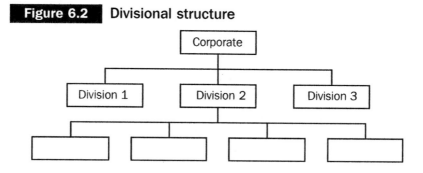

that the trend is to network organizations where dynamic processes and fluid teams replace rigid organizational lines. A matrix structure promotes knowledge sharing and collaboration that allow knowledge management to flourish. It enables coordination across both functions and products. It provides a flexible use of human resources across products and allows for integration within products. However, some of the weaknesses of this approach include high communication costs due to frequent and time-consuming meetings and coordination. It also requires people with good interpersonal communication skills and training.

Figure 6.3 Matrix structure

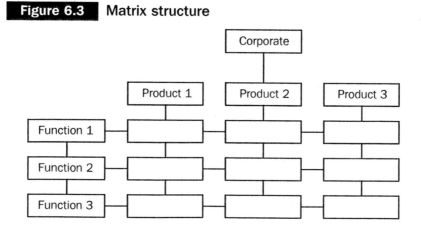

Leadership

Leadership has a great influence on organizational culture. In some cases culture is shaped by the ideas and beliefs of its leaders. Schein (1985) stated that both culture and leadership are two sides of the same coin: neither can really be understood by itself. He claims that there is a possibility that the most important thing – or the only thing – that a leader does is to create and manage culture. In a knowledge management context, management's commitment and continued support should be a prerequisite. McDermott and O'Dell (2001) noted in their findings that whether sharing knowledge is part of the business strategy or just part of the way of doing business, unambiguous support from direct managers is an important enabler of knowledge sharing. For example, in Buckman Labs, the CEO created a Knowledge Transfer Department and built K'Netix – a computer platform for sharing information. He appointed systems operators to monitor discussions in the forums and participated personally in the discussions. The management also provided substantial financial support to the whole process.

Trust

Organizational culture can be shaped by the level of trust between employees on the one hand, and between employees and management on the other. Mishra (1996) believes that trust is a multi-dimensional concept that includes belief in the good intent and concern of knowledge exchange partners, competence and capability, and belief in their reliability and their perceived openness. For knowledge sharing to happen, the contributor of knowledge needs to trust that his recipients will not misuse the knowledge and will give him the rightful credit, while the recipient has to trust the credibility, competence and good intent of the source of knowledge. An organization that practises fairness and transparency with regard to knowledge sharing fosters trust in its culture. A trustful environment will inadvertently encourage people to share their expertise and facilitate knowledge transfer and organizational learning.

Lack of trust, on the other hand, has a negative impact on the organizational culture and can lead to selfish practices and poor communication at all levels. According to Davenport and Prusak (1998), a high trust culture that promotes knowledge sharing should make trust visible, in that employees are given credit for sharing knowledge and the credit is evident. Trust must be ubiquitous, from the top to the bottom and across functions. An atmosphere of mutual trust must exist. If management exploit others' knowledge for personal gain, distrust will propagate throughout the company to the detriment of knowledge transfer.

Credibility and trustworthiness are important factors that affect knowledge management practices within the organization. Trust can be in a person, in the system, or in both. Interpersonal trust promotes social interaction and indirectly facilitates knowledge sharing. Hensen (1999) proposed a model of knowledge transfer where strong ties in the form of social interaction enhance the transfer of non-codified knowledge whereas weak ties allow the effective transfer of codified knowledge. Codified or explicit knowledge in the form of information does not require strong relationships or ties. Technology can be used to improve the information transfer process and the type of trust in this case might be based on professionalism and respect. This type of trust is referred to as cognitive trust when an individual believes that the trusted party has the experience or the qualifications to perform the job (McAllister, 1995). Non-codified knowledge or tacit knowledge, on the other hand, require different types of trust and need closer or stronger ties in the form of social relationships and lasting friendships. For an organization, it is much easier to institutionalize a certain level of trust that helps people to share explicit knowledge whereas it might not be able to engineer a trustworthy environment that ensures tacit knowledge transfer. The extent by which the organization can recognize the importance of social relationships will depend largely on the understanding of the value of tacit knowledge sharing and its role in the future development of the organization.

Reward, recognition, and motivation system

In order for trust and mutual respect to exist, a system of reward, recognition, and motivation must be present in the organization. Knowledge is something valuable and people might not give it away without something in return. The rewards and incentives system helps to shape the organizational culture. According to Smith and McKeen (2001), rewards and recognition relate positively to group cohesiveness, teamwork, performance, problem-solving, and problem-prevention. There are many forms of rewards. As pointed out by Beckman (1999), rewards include money, recognition, time off, empowerment, work selection, advancement, and development. Rewards should be early and often and they should promote desired behaviors, such as collaboration, experimentation, risk-taking, and learning. Unfortunately, more often than not, corporations tend to reward safe, bureaucratic behavior rather than risk-taking, individualistic behavior typical of innovators and entrepreneurship (Quinn, Baruch and Zien, 1997).

Zand (1997) pointed out that collaborative, integrative, win–win reward systems should be created in which one person's or organization's gain can also be a gain for their peers. He believes that collaborative rewards should be emphasized by linking bonuses to the overall profitability of the firm. Davenport and Prusak (1998) agree with Zand in that they believe management should evaluate performance based on sharing rather than rewarding only the knowledge owner. They even go a step further to suggest that the organization should practise rewarding creative errors. A knowledge-oriented reward system would then encourage members to share and collaborate in their daily course of work.

Informal networks and communities of practice

Knowledge sharing is best volunteered through social interaction in the informal networks, interest groups, and communities of practice which exist in almost every organization. Their existence is embraced and encouraged by some organizations, but discouraged and pushed underground by others. When employees lack the formal networks and platforms to express their opinion, they normally turn to informal networks and social groups to discuss issues which concern them. The approach different organizations take in tackling problems is a reflection of the organizational culture that facilitates or inhibits knowledge sharing. To what extent does the organization adopt working groups (consisting of people with different knowledge and experience) to solve problems? Does the organization allow informal networks and communities of practice to flourish? According to Nonaka and Takeuchi (1995), the existence of working groups is one of the necessary conditions for knowledge creation. Organizations with these types of practices benefit from a larger pool of ideas which prevents the groups from falling into the provision of routine solutions to problems. They cite the success of Matsushita in developing its first automatic bread-making machine by using the idea of a working group. Matsushita combined three product divisions with different subcultures, realizing that it needed the variety of knowledge possessed by the different groups. The new product combined the expertise in computer-control, experience with induction heater technology, and knowledge of rotating motors, and this collaboration of expertise brought the new product into fruition.

Social informal networks supplement and support formal organizational structure. Davenport and Prusak (1998) assert that informal networks move knowledge through the organization. Because they consist of people more or less continually in communication with one another, they tend to update themselves as conditions change. This is what we often refer to as gossip. Gossip constitutes a form of knowledge transfer about internal processes, it is the way the company's knowledge network updates itself. Self-organized groups or communities of practice facilitate knowledge sharing. Employees with similar interests, common work practices or aims gather and exchange ideas. They pool expertise and solve problems together. Members may come to develop trust over time, forming processes for sharing information and values, and engaging in symbiotic learning and teaching.

Cultural barriers

There are many cultural factors that inhibit knowledge sharing or knowledge transfer in the organization. Some of these factors are discussed below (see also Figure 6.1).

Asymmetry of knowledge

Asymmetry of knowledge takes place when knowledge does not flow from one part of the organization to another. In a normal situation, people in one department might not know that what they need is already available in the next department and they normally end up sourcing it somewhere else. Strategic and critical knowledge that resides in the minds of the top managers may not be accessible to the other managers for implementation purposes, resulting sometimes in uncertainty and confusion. Davenport and Prusak (1998) argue that tacit and ambiguous knowledge is especially hard to transfer from the resource that creates it to other parts of the organization.

One way to deal with this problem is job rotation, where staff spend time in different parts of the organization familiarizing themselves with different types of work and helping in the knowledge identification and management process. This also helps to facilitate the flow of information from one department to another. Encouraging interaction and communication among managers from different departments and with top management helps to promote knowledge transfer and knowledge sharing.

Lack of communication

Asymmetry of knowledge normally happens due to lack of communication between people in different departments or different segments of the population within the organization. Lack of communication can also come about as a result of the organizational structure affecting the style of work. For example, a heavy reliance on e-mails may limit the need for phone calls or face-to-face interaction between employees and senior management in the office. This may lead to the alienation of workers in the organization. Another factor may be too great an organizational emphasis on teamwork, leaving individuals feeling neglected which may result in staff not sharing their knowledge due to lack of recognition. Knowledge sharing needs to be voluntary and to take place in informal settings. Communication also need to be encouraged indirectly through programmes that will ensure that people are continuously talking about issues of concern to the organization.

Sharing reluctant cultures

Cultural issues take time to cultivate and instil in the organization. One of these is the culture that values knowledge sharing. While many organizations value knowledge creation and knowledge sharing, the vast majority of organizations possess cultures reluctant to share. Many organizations fail in trying to promote knowledge sharing because the knowledge-sharing approach does not match the organization's overall style. Cultural resistance to knowledge-sharing processes may be attributed to many factors, including lack of recognition, lack of communication, and a competitive environment where each individual is defined by his or her knowledge and achievements.

Knowledge-sharing activities within organizations vary a great deal in the approach and the methodology adopted. Some organizations recognize that knowledge sharing can only be volunteered and cannot be coerced and therefore create activities and cultivate a culture that values knowledge sharing. The formal knowledge-sharing activities created by some organizations may or may not work, depending on the many factors that govern the norms and practices within that organization. Based on their observations of different best-practice companies, McDermott and O'Dell (2001) state that 'the degree of formality, structure, physical resources, and language used to describe the effort matched the overall environment of each organization.'

Lack of incentives to share

Knowledge is a valuable resource and, as with any other type of asset, people will be very reluctant to give it away for free. Davenport and Prusak (1998) implied that people rarely share their knowledge without expecting something in return. This is common in a business climate where competition between employees is very stiff, and the monopolizing of knowledge by individuals may give them an edge over their peers. An obvious solution to this problem is to align the reward and recognition system with employees who support and adhere to the sharing of knowledge. Dermott and O'Dell (2001) maintain that reward and recognition is a way to make the importance of sharing knowledge visible.

Another method is to lead by example and highlight the benefits and impact of sharing. It is also important to highlight the dangers of monopolizing knowledge and that failing to build on the ideas of others has visible and sometimes serious career consequences. McDermott and O'Dell (2001) stated that 'because sharing knowledge is tied to a core value, an unwillingness to share is seen as more than just resistance to a new approach. Instead, it is seen as a direct violation of the core value to which knowledge sharing is linked' (p. 82).

Lack of focus

The absence of a clear organizational mission and business objectives might lead to failure in many knowledge management practices within the organization. McDermott and O'Dell (2001) pointed out three different ways to tie sharing knowledge to the business goals: first, make sharing knowledge directly part of the business strategy; secondly, piggyback sharing knowledge onto another key business initiative; and thirdly, share knowledge routinely as the way we work.

Since knowledge sharing most of the time takes place between people who share common values or business objectives, there is a need for the organization to articulate, emphasize, and aggregate the need to share knowledge by building it into the core values of the organization. Building core values as well as clear business objectives enables employees to focus on the issues that concern the organization and will enable them to relate to the way these business objectives can be achieved.

Communication and resistance to change

Most people understand the importance of organizational culture in ensuring the successful implementation of knowledge management in general and knowledge sharing in particular. Communication plays an important role in ensuring the success of any change in the organizational culture. Communicating the right message to the right people at the right time through the right channels within the organization is crucial to the success of any cultural change (Al-Hawamdeh, 2002). Communicating for organizational change largely depends on the mix of reasons for the change itself and the sources of possible resistance. According to Conner (1998), some of the crucial success factors for change management include commitment from senior management, the nature and intensity of resistance to change, the culture of the organization, and the knowledge and skill of the change agents, those who help to execute the change.

The transformation of the organizational culture is impossible unless people in the organization are willing to participate and help. Kotter (1996) stated that 'people will not make sacrifices ... unless they think that the potential benefits of change are attractive and unless they really believe that transformation is possible. Without credible communication, and a lot of it, employees' minds and hearts are never captured' (p. 9). Many organizations today understand that knowledge cannot be treated as an organizational asset without the active and voluntary participation of the communities that are its true owners (Snowden, 2000). The question of how to convince the staff to volunteer their knowledge and remain relevant is a challenging one. Many organizations prefer to coerce employees to share their knowledge through a series of rigid policies. This is no longer possible as employees today have higher expectations, form their own values and perceptions, and therefore are more resistant to any change that they view as not beneficial to their welfare.

Changing the mindset of the people in the organization through communicating the rationale for the need to change is very important. Oliver (1997) explained that firms that cannot control their employees' hearts can at least attempt to influence their souls through internal lobbying, mission statements and, occasionally, codes of ethics and value statements. Although communication may not change people, it may at least remove the barriers to change. It is also essential to communicate upwards as well as downwards in order to trigger positive employee involvement so as to harness their expertise. Communication strategies can help to reduce the negativity expressed toward change and the implementation of knowledge management within the organization. Al-Hawamdeh (2002) discusses a communication strategy framework that consists of three phases: the preparation stage, the mobilization phase and the implementation phase. The framework also includes five stages or steps to acceptance and commitment based on the communication escalator proposed by Quirke (1995).

Figure 6.4 shows the communication strategy framework and the five acceptance and commitment stages or steps. The first step in the communication strategy is to raise awareness among the staff and management within the organization. The second step is to create an understanding of the benefits of knowledge management practices and the rationale for the organizational cultural change. The shift from awareness to understanding is open to feedback and additional information tailored to the needs of a more closely defined group of people. Communication may be more face to face and more interactive. The aim here is not simply to present messages but to provide a rationale, get feedback, and refine communication until the message gets through. It will also focus on getting feedback to check for understanding. Such processes could include management conferences and customer feedback forums.

Figure 6.4 **Communication strategy framework**

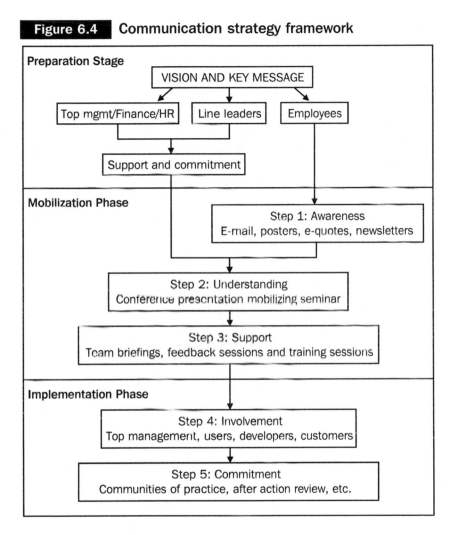

The third step is getting the support of the staff for the proposed changes. It is not enough to get people to understand what is happening and what its implications will be. The aim is to solicit acceptance, if not of the change itself, then of the need for and the rationale behind the change. The focus will be more on education than presentation, with input from outside the organization and a review of parallel trends in other industries and the changing dynamics of the business. Such sessions could include business forums, training events, and customer seminars.

The fourth step is to get staff involved through their participation in the various knowledge-sharing sessions and training. The aim here is to get employees to share their pre-existing reactions, concerns, and objections, as well as to provide them with management thinking. These processes will be far more of a dialogue, with the aim of sharing thinking, assessing implications, exploring alternatives, and reviewing the best means of implementation.

The fifth step is to build commitment and ownership by the target audience through communication of the need for change, and the goals and direction of the change. Commitment comes from a sense of ownership and having participated in the development of the strategy and solution.

Organization culture can have a negative impact on knowledge management practices. It can be an enabler and at the same time an inhibitor of knowledge management initiatives. However, in cases where the organizational culture acts as a barrier, is it possible to change it? Studies have shown that, despite the fact that culture is deep-rooted in the organization, it can be changed (Schein, 1985; Duffy, 1999; Long, 1997). Smith and McKeen (2001) stated that it is precisely the fact that culture is dynamic and changes over time that makes pinning down what is culture difficult and therefore challenging to leaders. More specifically, Long (1997) defines culture in terms of values, norms, and practices. He argues that values are deeply embedded and contain tacit assumptions that are difficult to articulate. It is too complex and difficult to change. However, norms and practices are more observable and easier to identify, thus are more amenable to change. Practices are the most visible, providing the most direct levers for changing the behaviors needed to support knowledge management practices.

Based on the premise that culture is changeable, Schein (1985) believes that leaders need to lead the change. Long (1997) agrees that leaders need to drive the KM strategy personally when it comes to changing the organization's values. They have to believe strongly that there is a need to change the values and are willing to lead a long-term change project lasting years. Long further pointed out that changing the practices that generate behavior is the most direct way to change behavior and thus alter the organizational norms which will reinforce the necessary behaviors over time. New behaviors resulting from new practices will change norms over time, providing long-term support for more effective knowledge use.

7

Communities of practice

Introduction

Due to the complex nature of knowledge, we can always argue that we are all engaged in knowledge management activities in one way or another. But the real issue in my opinion is not so much whether we are practising knowledge management or not, but rather how good we are at it. The same can be said about communities of practice. Communities of practice are everywhere. They are in schools and universities, in work and at home, in sports and so on. Again the issue is not whether we belong to communities of practice or not, but on whether we are aware of their importance and the benefits they bring to the organization.

Communities of practice are about people. They normally develop around things that matter to them. It is the realization of the importance of what they are doing that distinguishes one community from the others. Sometimes those issues that concern the community have an impact on the well-being of the whole community. In the case of an organization, it will translate into an organizational asset that can help shape the future of the organization as a whole. According to Wenger, communities of practice are groups of people who share a common concern, a set of problems or a passion about a topic, and who deepen their knowledge and expertise in this area by interacting on an ongoing basis (Wenger, McDermott and Snyder 2002). Stamp (2000) highlighted that learning is social and happens on the job.

Through interactions via storytelling, mentoring and discussions, communities of practice allow the better transfer of tacit knowledge. Many of the skills and competencies acquired in the job environment are through observation and training. Within communities of practice people share common values, observe and interact with each other, exchange views and ideas and contribute to the knowledge creation process. Knowledge creation and transfer are integral parts of communities of practice activities and interaction. Communities of practice are not just a means of constructing a repository of information, but take it one step further by learning what this information means, what its limits are and how it can be used. Such a manner of learning is not restricted to theory but applied in practice to the real world. Ward (2000) made an interesting analogy between these communities and a garden which must be tendered and nurtured for all the plants to grow and blossom. He believes that communities of practice have the potential to enhance the organization's ability to learn and grow and in return form the organization's most versatile and dynamic knowledge resource.

Characteristics of communities of practice

The characteristics of communities of practice vary from one organization to another. They vary in the form they can take as well as in the manner of practice. Communities of practice start over a common interest, certain problems that concern a group of people, or as a result of sharing certain values and beliefs. The people who belong to these communities might not be working together everyday, but they meet in either a physical or virtual space because they find value in their interactions. Through discussion, interaction, and participation, they share information, insight, and advice, and help each other in solving common problems. People working in organizations often develop such informal networks of relationships that indirectly promote knowledge sharing. Informal networks of relationships often enable the organization to accomplish tasks faster and better. Figure 7.1 shows some of the characteristics of communities of practice.

Figure 7.1 Characteristics of communities of practice

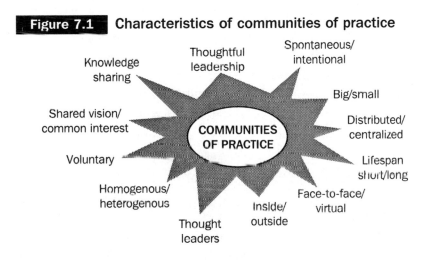

Most communities of practice emerge spontaneously, without any effort on the part of management. The members get together voluntarily for a common purpose where they can learn from each other. The informal nature of many communities of practice creates a more conducive environment for knowledge sharing. The members in these communities share equal amounts of passion and commitment to the issues being raised and discussed. The community of 'Turbodudes' from Shell, for example, largely made up of experts interested in turbidite structures, was formed to discuss and resolve the issues that arise in their course of work (Wenger, McDermott, and Synder, 2002). Initially, communities of practice may not be recognized in the organization and are responsible for themselves (Stewart, 1996). However, Wenger raised the possibility of communities being incorporated into the official structure of the organization once their deliverables are found to be valuable. Ward (2000) further pointed out that, without any formal guidance, the potential benefits of the community may not be fully tapped and directed towards the strategic needs of the company. However, this may inhibit the growth of such communities.

There are many different types of communities of practice. Some are closely knit groups of specialists who share knowledge via informal and unstructured discussions, while some occasionally seek out others for advice and information. Hence the size of a community can vary from a few participants to a few hundred people. The size is important, as it will determine the structure of the community as well as how the activities are carried out. The development of a community takes time, but its lifespan again varies widely. Some communities of practice can exist for centuries such as communities of artisans, while others can be as short as a few years.

There are a number of reasons for the short lifespan of a community. One is the topic or the area of interest, which might become obsolete and as a result the lifespan of the community may come to an end. Another factor that might affect the lifespan of the community is the scope or the domain. If the domain fails to inspire the community members, the growth and even the overall lifespan of the community will be affected. Time constraints, trust among members, and support from the management if the community of practice is a formal arrangement are also factors that may affect the lifespan and continuity of the community.

Technology facilitates the creation of communities of practice by people from different organizations, different countries, and even different industries. Today communities can transcend geographical boundaries, especially with the impact of globalization. For example, the IBM Consulting Group employed Intellectual Capital Management (ICM) as part of the company's re-engineering project. The idea is to institutionalize a formal community throughout IBM Global Services and Global Industries. The efforts culminated in the creation of ICM AssetWeb, a dynamic Lotus Notes-based collaboration system that gives practitioners in IBM Global Services the power to leverage intellectual capital (Huang, 1998). The use of technology enhances communication and enables people to share information and exchange ideas. However, it is important to emphasize that online interaction is not sufficient for communities of practice as technology tools will not be able to substitute entirely for face-to-face interaction and create the level of trust that normally develops in a real community. Although online tools can greatly enhance communication and cohesion, they do not by themselves constitute a community. Face-to-face events are vital, particularly in creating trust and cementing the relationships within the community.

Communities of practice are about knowledge sharing. The best way to share knowledge is through social interaction and informal learning processes such as storytelling, conversation, coaching, and apprenticeship. All these processes can be found in communities of practice. However, the types of activities held by different communities differ. Some conduct face-to-face discussion regularly, while others interact in virtual space using e-mail, discussion boards, video conferencing, online chat, etc. In a community of practice, the members participate voluntarily and assume roles to support one another. The roles may be formal or informal. Wenger (2002) identified some roles, namely the community coordinators, experts and 'thought leaders,' pioneers and administrators. Community coordinators and thought leaders are the key to the community's success. The community leader is a member who helps the community focus on its domain, maintains interrelationships, develops its practice and even creates a bridge between the community and the formal organization. The 'thought leaders' are usually those well-seasoned and well-respected practitioners of the defined domain, and hence attract potential members. Other members also play their roles by identifying issues or problems that crop up in the course of their work for discussion and sourcing for relevant information.

It is also important to differentiate between communities of practice, interest groups, and project teams. Table 7.1 shows the difference between the three different categories. Interest groups and communities of practice are very similar in the way they emerge and form over a period of time. The major difference between both communities is the level of commitment and focus. Interest group members tend to be diverse in nature and share a common interest without much commitment and conviction. Communities of practice are people who share a common interest and develop chemistry and lasting friendship. Project teams, on the other hand, are task oriented and management assigns the members. The group is heterogeneous and the focus is more on deliverables rather than knowledge creation.

Value of communities of practice

The value of a community of practice is measured by its contribution to the knowledge-creation process. What makes communities of practice valuable is their ability to promote knowledge sharing through socialization. Communities of practice create value for their members and their organization and in return they contribute to success in the knowledge economy. Figure 7.2 shows the importance of communities of practice in innovation and business processes. Knowledge sharing that takes place within the community results in innovation and product development. All these activities normally happen in a continuous learning environment.

Table 7.1 — Communities of practice in relation to interest groups and project teams

Aspect	Communities of practice	Interest groups	Project teams
Communication	Face to face, IT	Face to face, IT	Face to face, IT
Goals	Knowledge sharing, learning, knowledge creation	Knowledge sharing, learning, knowledge creation	Task, project oriented
Culture	Culture of learning	Culture of learning	Culture of action
Emergence	Spontaneous	Spontaneous	Intentional
Administration	Voluntary, informal	Voluntary, informal	Formal
Knowledge need	Community	Individual	Project requirements
Knowledge use	Individual, group, organization	Individual, group	Individual, group
Duration/lifespan	Unlimited, short/long	Unlimited, short/long	Limited
Membership	Core members, voluntary	Membership open	Membership assigned
Structure	Homogeneous	Heterogeneous	Heterogeneous
Focus	Same topics, same problems, same interest	Mixed topics, different problems, same interest	Deliverables

Figure 7.2 — The value of communities of practice

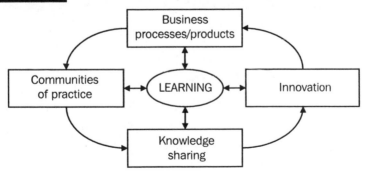

Value to the individuals

As with any other professional activity where the returns are not immediate, communities of practice create value for its individual members in many ways. In the short term, when members encounter problems in their work, they are able to get immediate help from other community members. Hence there is easy access to the relevant expertise and less time is required to hunt for information or solutions. With constant interactions in the community and exposure to the different perspectives of their peers, the members are able to devise better solutions and make better decisions. The knowledge they acquire through participation in the community will enhance their skill and competencies resulting in a better performance at work. Members also tend to become more confident in their approach to problem-solving. A good example is the community of practice in Xerox for IT professionals. It provides a means for them to manage their complex infrastructure more effectively. They are better able to provide high-quality, validated solutions to unstructured problems and deal with the never-ending new developments in hardware and software (Storck and Hill, 2000). Storck further noted that the motivation for learning and developing at an individual level seemed greater in this type of community structure than in other organizational forms. On a long-term basis, this has important implications for the performance of these individuals, as members are able to keep abreast of new developments in their field. This is even more important in the IT-related field where technology advances at a fast pace.

Value to the organization

With the increased emphasis on knowledge and intangible assets, communities of practice are becoming recognized as valuable organizational assets. The value created and the knowledge gained by individual members can now be seen as relevant and beneficial to the whole organization. Communities of practice can be an integral part of the organization and they play an important role in research and development activities. The community can be viewed as an arena where the members are able to find answers for specific problems, raise questions and get answers in a quicker and efficient way. With multiple perspectives and collective knowledge, a complex problem can be simplified and overcome. Although the traditional way of documentation also caters for the sharing of knowledge, that knowledge frequently remains unused and not up to date. With communities of practice, the organization is able to come up with the best solution in a shorter time and at lower cost. And the collective knowledge generated is 'shared' by all the communities' members. In addition, the organization is also able to respond more rapidly to customer needs and inquiries with improved quality (Storck and Hill, 2000).

For most organizations, the learning curve for new employees is a cost and productivity issue. It is important for the new employees to get acquainted with the procedures, methodology, tools and activities involved in the new position. An effective form of learning normally happens on the job and through interaction with fellow workers. The interaction with the communities of practice in the organization minimizes the amount of time needed for training and lessens the impact on the workflow. According to Lesser and Storck (2001), communities of practice enable the new employees to pick up the organizational navigation knowledge and ease the task of learning both the technical and cultural aspects of the new roles and responsibilities. Wenger (1998) also added that communities of practice are able to retain knowledge in a living way through frequent discussions, unlike a database or a manual. Moreover, the communities preserve the tacit aspects of knowledge that formal systems cannot capture. Therefore new employees are able to learn better and faster from the experiences of their seniors.

Stimulating and encouraging innovation is one of the main advantages of communities of practice. Communities of practice provide the platform needed for the exchange of ideas and discussions about similar problems and likely solutions. Brailsford (2001) pointed out that communities are able to create the cultural environment ideal for innovation by stimulating interactions and connecting members with overlapping skills and disciplines. The members discuss novel ideas, work together on problems, and keep up with development in the industry. Many of the informal discussions and activities within the communities of practice are normally a form of brainstorming and answer-seeking. With such rich discussions of the different perspectives and experiences, the likelihood of innovative ideas emerging increases, spawning new products and services. When the communities of practice keep abreast of market opportunities and their own practice developments, in the long term they can even formulate new strategic initiatives and best practices relevant to the organization.

Communities of practice help shape the organization landscape. They provide a sense of identity to their members in the members' workplace, no matter to which team they belong. A good community of practice is one that values its members and always looks to them as key contributors to the knowledge and memory of the community. Wenger (1998) stated that 'in a sea of information, it helps us sort out what we pay attention to, what we participate in, and what we stay away from.' Having a sense of identity is a crucial aspect of learning in the organization.

People in the organization are normally formed into small informal networking groups which are very similar to communities of practice. Their loyalty to a smaller group tends to be stronger than to the organization as a whole. Nurturing these informal groups into communities of practice and aligning their mission with that of the organization will create more bonding and a greater sense of belonging. Making people feel more comfortable and recognized within small groups will help to increase the retention of talent in the organization.

It will also attract good and more capable people who feel that their presence is welcomed and their contributions are highly appreciated in the community. In the event of loss of personnel from the organization, the loss of knowledge or 'brain drain' is greatly minimized as this knowledge is living within the community. In order to fully benefit from the employees' innovations, the organization must support the communities and help them develop their identities.

Evolution of communities of practice

Like all other living things, communities have to go through a cycle of birth, growth, ageing, and death. The longer a community of practice can be sustained is an indication of the healthy state of mind of that community. The contributions the community makes to innovation and science can be measured by the level of interaction within the community, the lifespan of the community and the products and services generated by the people within the communities. Wenger, McDermott, and Snyder in 2002 proposed a community evolution model based on the life-cycle perspective, describing communities as developing through stages similar to birth, maturation, and death. They see communities of practice as progressing through five stages: potential, coalescing, active, dispersed, and memorable. The communities start off as loose networks with the potential to become more connected. As members build connections, a community of practice is formed. Members' interaction within the community generally increases through the active level, experiencing cycles of high and low activity. However, it is during this stage that the process of learning is at its peak. Then it declines through the dispersed stage, and finally disappears at the memorable level, leaving behind memories and stories for the community members.

One important point to remember is that, unlike other projects where the organization can decide when and where to start, it is not possible to dictate the start of a community of practice or who the members making up that community will be. However, the organization can help to nurture communities that already exist or are likely to be formed naturally. The birth of a community can take a long time, and the people making up that community may also take time to discover that they belong to it. McDermott (2000) views communities as living, human institutions that form spontaneously, grow, mature, change, age, and die. He uses this life-cycle concept to describe the five stages of community development in a similar way to Wenger's model but with more elaboration of the tensions and challenges that stimulate the community in development, but that eventually lead to the community's death.

IBM Global Services started a project in 1995 aimed at providing support for the growth and development of communities of practice which focused on the competencies of the organization (Gongla and Rizzuto, 2001). The model describes how communities transform themselves, becoming more capable at each stage while at the same time maintaining a distinct, coherent identity. The five stages outlined in the project include: potential, building, engaged, active, and adaptive. The first stage signifies the formation of the community which progresses to a more definite structure and direction. As the community grows in size in the engaged stage, it starts to learn to adjust, improve, and leverage on its knowledge. At the active stage, the community begins to understand and benefit from the knowledge management processes as well as the collective work of the community. In the last level, the community moves to the stage of using knowledge for competitive advantage, bringing immense benefit to the organization.

It is clear from the three models discussed above that communities of practice evolve in a unique way and can also vary according to the situation. A community can move forward and evolve from one stage to another or stay stagnant at a particular stage and finally dissolve without evolving to another level. On the other hand, a community may remain dormant for extended periods of time at one stage but suddenly 'awaken' and progress to the next level. The level at which a community belongs is determined by how similar its characteristics are to those of that particular level. However, especially at transitional periods for example, the community may actually manifest the traits of another stage. All in all, the life-cycle of a community can be very unpredictable.

The evolution of communities of practice can be affected by many factors, including people, technology, and culture, and their impact varies from one environment to another. The people, technology, and culture also need to be considered as a whole. It is difficult to expect that it will help if people and culture are not contributing to the evolution of the community. The active participation of community members encourages innovation, individual growth, and problem-solving. Furthermore, the emergence of internal leadership in each community is also important. As the community grows, it will mature to the next level.

Fostering communities of practice

Communities of practice are informal groupings that can take many forms across departments within the same organization or even across geographical boundaries. The benefits these groupings bring to the individual members, as well as to the organization fostering these communities, is tremendous. Management of organizations wanting to embark on communities of practice initiatives must understand that communities of practice are informal grouping that emerge spontaneously and cannot be controlled or created overnight. The management role in fostering communities of practice is more one of facilitating the process and supporting its growth and development. It is important to maintain a balance if the organization hopes to gain the benefits of communities of practice without killing them with red tape and constraints.

Effective communication, mutual understanding and trust are other important factors in fostering communities of practice. Organizations need to foster trust and team spirit among the employees, as well as teach them interaction and networking skills. Creating an environment for social activism among employees serves as a stepping stone for the development of communities of practice. Organizations should try to avoid documenting everything and as a result creating stockpiles of underutilized information or, in other words, 'information junkyards.' To leverage knowledge effectively, communities of practice need to understand what type of knowledge is strategically important to the business (McDermott, 1999). It will be useful if management highlight their goals and organizational directions to their employees directly.

It is wrong for an organization to assume that sharing information is the same as sharing knowledge. Sharing insights and experience within a community is not simply a matter of transmitting information via e-mails, web pages or minutes of meetings. People in the organization need to be aware that the information will be useful: it needs to be translated from the context in which it was developed to the context in which it will be applied. What one person considers valuable to share will depend on his/her experience, goals, problems, and interests. Similarly, what another person considers as useful in his or her workplace depends on his or her experience, goals, problems, and interests. It is important to ensure common understanding of the information communicated through frequent interaction and regular discussions.

One of the most difficult tasks in knowledge management is for an organization to ensure that tacit knowledge in the form of skills and competencies can be passed from one employee in the organization to another. Since tacit knowledge is a form of hidden knowledge that even the owner of the knowledge is not aware of, the only way to share that knowledge is through people-to-people activities such as storytelling, discussions, observations, and on-the-job training. Informal communities of practice play an important role in this knowledge-sharing process. This is because, through interaction, people build enough common contexts to understand each other and enough trust to be willing to share ideas and provide freely what normally people consider to be very valuable.

Given the important role communities of practice play in knowledge sharing, it is important to design an interaction format that promotes openness and allows for informal networks to develop. The community coordinator and leaders should try to address issues of interest to community members built around a flexible agenda and allowing for greater input from the members. The format should provide enough time for social interaction and exchange of ideas. Technology can and should be used to assist in connecting remote members to enable them to take part in the discussion and exchange of ideas. To further foster the bond among the community members, special events such as conferences, seminars, technology or trade fairs, social gatherings, brainstorming events, etc. can be held from time to time.

While technology can be used to assist in maintaining community-mindedness, technology alone is insufficient for effective community development. Technology plays an important role in enabling knowledge sharing and facilitating interaction between members within the community, especially when members travel from or live in different geographical locations. The management role is also important in fostering communities of practice. Although many communities of practice emerge without any interventions from management, management can facilitate and encourage people to participate in such communities. Wenger, McDermott, and Snyder (2002) state: 'A plant does its growing, whether its seed was carefully planted or blown into place by the wind... However, you can do much to encourage healthy plants: till the soil, ensure they have enough nutrients, supply water...'

The organization can provide the rich soil for communities of practice to grow in. With the intention of fostering communities of practice in various part of the organization, management should be more understanding of employees devoting the time and effort to participate in such activities and value learning and of the need for employees to engage in these activities. Trust is one of the key elements in fostering any community, and management need to have more trust in employees and their abilities to manage both work schedules and community activities. Sometimes an organization perceives people to be of a higher caliber and is prepared to pay them large sums of money in terms of salary but still refuse to trust them to do the job and give them the necessary space to balance the job and self-development. Participating in communities of practice is a form of self-development that impacts significantly on the knowledge-sharing and knowledge-creation process within the organization. Creating the right environment or the right organizational culture will encourage employees to take part in communities of practice and actively engage in their activities, yet still be able to perform well in their jobs.

Offering incentives or awards as a form of recognition and encouragement for community members is another way of indirectly fostering the creation and maintainability of communities of practice. Community members who come up with innovative ideas or best practices relevant to the organization can be rewarded. However, we should be careful when providing incentives and recognition. The rewards should be given to communities of practice that started spontaneously and became successful. If people come to know that rewards are given for starting communities of practice, then people might start communities just for the sake of getting the reward and the communities become artificial in nature and lack the elements of trust and sincerity.

8

The learning organization and organizational learning

Introduction

It is difficult to distinguish between the learning organization and organizational learning. Ang and Joseph (1996) carried out a study to compare organizational learning and the learning organization in terms of process versus structure. McGill et al. (1992), on the other hand, did not distinguish between the learning organization and organizational learning. They defined organizational learning as the ability of an organization to gain insight and understanding from experience through experimentation, observation, and analysis, and through a willingness to examine both successes and failures. Organizational learning can be viewed as the process of gaining knowledge and developing skills and competencies which enable the organization to compete more effectively. Learning can take place individually, collectively as a team, or as an organization. Although learning is always considered an individual activity, organizations as a whole are facing increased competition and see organizational learning as a key to their survival. Duffy (1999) links learning and knowledge and considers them the basis for innovation, productivity, and performance. He identifies knowledge, learning, innovation, productivity, and performance as the drivers of business success where each needs the support of strategy, people, processes, and technology. Learning from past experience, processes, and practices leads to the creation of knowledge and the generation of new ideas and new concepts which can then be applied to improve the organization's productivity and performance and to develop innovative products. The new knowledge created can be used as an input for future learning.

The concept of the learning organization is neither easy to define nor distinguish from organizational learning. Senge (1990) defined learning organizations as '...organizations where people continually expand their capacity to create the results they truly desire, where new expansive patterns of thinking are nurtured, where collective aspiration is set free, and where people are continually learning how to learn together.' Bennett and O'Brien (1994) believe that a learning organization is one that has woven a continuous and enhanced capacity to learn, adapt, and change into the fabric of its character, and emphasize that the learning organization has values, policies, programs, and structures that support and accelerate organizational learning.

Successful organizations are committed to learning as a way to ensure knowledge transfer in the form of skills and competencies. Knowledge transfer can be carried out through sharing, collaboration, and teamwork, and through the development of the ability to exploit and learn from what they know. Hamel and Prahalad (1994) pointed out that a firm has abundant experiences as every day employees interact with new customers, learn about competitors, think about new solutions, and debate various organizational issues. The difference between firms is measured not just by the relative quality or depth of their stockpile of experiences but by their relative capacity to derive learning from those experiences. Though employees possess a wealth of knowledge and experience about their organization, products, customers, practices, and competitors, individuals or departments of the organization hold much of this knowledge in isolation.

The learning processes within the organization have to be fostered. It is important to understand what triggers or impedes learning and sharing. The learning process must be both efficient and closely integrated with work, as knowledge workers will have difficulty fitting learning into their professional and personal lives. There is a need to integrate content from many resources, extract new knowledge from work and bring learning to the workplace via appropriate information technologies (Lytle, 1999). Forming teams that allow debate, challenges, and creative tension to occur is one way to encourage learning and the generation of new knowledge. Team members will be exposed to different perspectives, learn from other members and interpret and use shared knowledge appropriately. It is the collective ability of employees to apply knowledge in innovative ways that provides continuous strategic renewal to an organization.

Organizational knowledge and organizational activities tend to vary from one department to another. Sometimes, knowledge specialization develops by product division, business function, and department. This gives rise to problems in the coordination of activities and the integration of specialized knowledge located in different organizational units which is necessary to build strategic capabilities. Bessant and Pavitt (1997) observed that internal structures and processes must continuously balance two conflicting requirements. The first is to be able to identify and develop specialized knowledge within the technological fields, business functions, and product divisions. The second requirement is to be able to exploit this knowledge through integration across technological fields, business functions, and product divisions. Due to this conflict, it is necessary to strategically manage knowledge and to look for integration across the organization. Internal integration relates to the linking of specialized skills, knowledge bases, and technological and managerial systems. External integration relates to the generation of options using external sources of information and to the ability to evaluate those options according to the existing knowledge base.

Two sides of the same coin

Knowledge management practices are key enablers and essential tools for a learning organization. They provide the needed infrastructure in the form of information, systems and processes that facilitate the management of knowledge and flow of information within the organization. The concepts of the learning organization and knowledge management can be considered as two sides of the same coin. Skyrme (2000) pointed out that Anglian Water in the UK made knowledge, innovation, and learning the key levers of customer services in its organizational learning programmes. The move facilitated its successful transition from a regional utility to a globally oriented business. He also pointed out that Glaxo Wellcome captured and harnessed the knowledge of its scientists through a learning organization program that resulted in the adoption of knowledge networking techniques. Probst, Raub, and Romhardt (1999) argued that knowledge management could be seen as a further development of the concept of organizational learning. The key focus is to improve organizational skills at all levels in the organization through better handling of the knowledge resources.

Knowledge management can be seen as an essential activity within the context of the learning organization. After all, an effective learning process will require knowledge identification, transfer, and sharing. Knowledge creation or organizational learning occurs best in groups of people that are deeply engaged in getting something done which is challenging their present level of capabilities (Karlenzig, 1999). Increasingly, researchers and practitioners view learning as a social activity and people learn best when they can interact with other people as full members in communities of shared interest (Rosenberg, 2001). In this respect organizations need to provide a cooperative and collaborative environment in which employees learn from each other as well as from both mistakes and successes, and new ideas emerge as a result of the increased interaction. Access to the right information at the right time, a sense of belonging and trust in the knowledge community are necessary for learning to take place.

Through proper planning and development, knowledge management can be used as a tool to foster communities of practice, encourage knowledge-sharing activities, and manage content. It is a challenge to manage tacit knowledge or try to capture it in any form other than by encouraging people to communicate and learn from each other. Knowledge management involves e-learning that can be used to deal with time management problems. E-learning combined with some face-to-face interaction from time to time can be a very effective way of learning. Practices in knowledge management are now shifting from strategies that focus on dissemination to those that promote education and innovation (McElroy, 1999). Knowledge management is not only focused on capturing explicit factual information, but is also focused on the experiences and learning of individual employees. The development of knowledge management models now considers how they can be used to support business, create and add value to knowledge, and support organizational learning. Evolving the knowledge management strategy from the concept of organizational learning will lead to more innovation and higher efficiency, and help the organization transform itself into a high-performance learning organization.

The importance of learning

Learning is a basic process by which static information is transformed into dynamic or active information. It is a skill that we possess intrinsically and continue to use throughout our lives, whether in the workplace or elsewhere. Liebowitz (1998) defined learning as the acquisition and application of new knowledge, skills, and experiences that change behavior, thought, and beliefs to improve performance or to better adapt to or to take advantage of the environment. In the knowledge economy, failure to learn in the organization could spell disaster. Many researchers and practitioners argue that organizations should continue to invest in learning to ensure the transfer of knowledge that will help in sustaining the business. The flow of information and know-how within the organization facilitates knowledge creation and knowledge sharing which in return improves productivity and enhances organizational competitive advantage.

Learning activities in an organization may take place in a planned or unplanned manner by individuals or groups within the organization. Learning sources, whether internal or external, are plentiful and these are in the form of self-learning, competitors, experts, industry, environment, corporate memory, etc. Given the importance of learning, according to Garvin (2000) learning processes have to be analysed to foster better learning and they have to be 'managed' so that more effective learning occurs by design rather than by chance.

The changes brought about by the information and knowledge society have had a great impact on the learning process. The changes in work patterns and mobility and the increased emphasis on skills and competencies demand that workers and knowledge professionals adopt learning as a survival tool. Traditionally, job demands focus attention primarily on task performance but knowledge workers are now assessed by the results they achieve in work with a high level of knowledge content. The changing nature of work could also result in less opportunity for learning as knowledge workers can be geographically dispersed and spend most of their time solving today's urgent issues rather than learning for tomorrow's. Taking into account these issues the learning processes need to be both efficient through the use of technology and effective through close integration with work rather than stand as a separate activity.

Many authors believe that it is important to distinguish between organizational learning and the learning organization. According to Dibella and Nevis (1997), the learning organization is a systems-level concept with particular characteristics for the preferred organization. In contrast, organizational learning describes certain types of learning activities or processes that may occur at the individual, team, or organizational level. Thus organizational learning is something that occurs in all organizations whereas the learning organization is a particular type or form of organization. The learning style is a characteristic that an organization exhibits in addressing its improvement. Three different styles of learning are discussed in the literature. These are single-loop, double-loop and deutero learning.

Single-loop learning

Single-loop learning refers to the detection and correction of errors (Argyris and Schon, 1996). This is the basic level of organizational learning where the effectiveness of the rules and policies is questioned. However, single-loop learning can be detrimental to the learning organization as it can create a 'competency trap' because organizations become less likely to seek alternatives (Levitt and March, 1988).

Double-loop learning

This type of learning is more in-depth and occurs when the organization is willing to look at deeper organizational norms and structures, to raise questions about their validity, and to look at why the errors or successes occurred in the first place (Marquardt, 1996). This results in fundamental changes that might impact values, strategies and beliefs. Hence, double-loop learning can be seen as trying to solve the root causes of a problem and not the symptoms. Single-loop learning is important for solving immediate problems and getting the 'everyday job done' whereas double-loop learning is necessary for the organization to have 'another day' (Argyris and Schon, 1996). It is argued that double-loop learning is more likely to lead to the organization gaining competitive advantage than single-loop learning (Slater and Narver, 1995). However, Schein (1993) stresses that most organizations and individuals are unwilling to engage in double-loop learning because it involves the disclosure of errors and mistakes as well as the questioning of existing assumptions, norms, structures, and processes.

Deutero learning

Argyris and Schon (1996) called this 'learning about learning'. Enterprises that nurture the deutero learning style enquire not only into the root causes and outcomes of their practices which double-loop actions attempt to uncover, but also explore the relevance of their whole learning process. Members discover what they did that eased or inhibited learning; they invent new strategies for learning in order to generate or innovate the learning process. The results are encoded and reflected in organizational learning practice.

The successful organization is multi-layered and moves through the three successive styles progressively. However, the effectiveness of the organization as a learning organization lies not so much in progressing through the stages, but is more about the speed at which it reaches a higher stage (Lassey, 1998; Kline and Saunders, 1993).

The fundamentals of a learning organization

While the concept of a learning organization is still evolving, learning organizations are based on several ideas and principles that determine how individuals within the organization interact and inter-organizational practices are carried out. Senge (1990) visualizes the learning organization as continually expanding its capacity to create its future. For such an organization, it is not enough merely to survive. Survival learning or adaptive learning is necessary, but for a learning organization, the adaptive learning has to be joined by generative learning or double-loop learning that enhances the capacity to create. Here lies the potential of the learning organization to introduce significant changes, not just a great volume of incremental, adaptive changes. According to Senge, what fundamentally distinguishes learning organizations from traditional bureaucratic organizations will be mastery of five basic disciplines – personal mastery, mental models, shared vision, team learning, and systems thinking, as shown in Figure 8.1.

Figure 8.1 Senge's five components of a learning organization

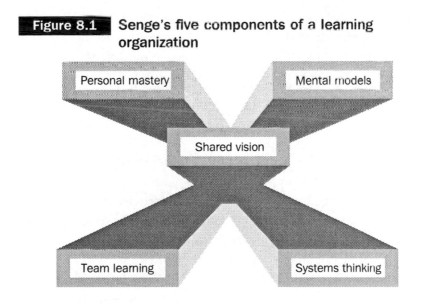

Mental models

Mental models to a large extent determine our perception of the world around us. We form them to help us to see the world in a simplified manner. They allow individuals within the organization to think about and reflect upon the structure and direction of the organization. They can also be viewed as filters and simplified mechanisms to deal with complex problems. Often, new ideas and insights conflict with deeply held beliefs making it difficult for these ideas to get into practice. These predefined beliefs and perceptions of the world can often limit individuals to familiar ways of thinking and acting. According to Senge (1990), the problem with an existing mental model is not whether it is right or wrong but that it lies beneath one's consciousness and, therefore, is extremely difficult to identify and in turn examine. By not examining or questioning our underlying beliefs we run the risk of never moving forward. Relying on our perception of the world and operating from our assumptions will never allow new and better ideas to surface. A learning organization needs to be aware of the existence of mental models and be willing to examine and challenge them. A climate of cooperation can be created through shared mental models if everyone wishes the firm to develop in the same way.

Shared vision

Shared vision enables people within the organization to look at the world through the same magnifying glass. It implies a sense of group commitment to a set of goals and objectives. It is the ability to create a sense of belonging and the ability to bind people together around a common identity and sense of destiny. Shared vision is important to the organization as it provides a focus and creates a reference point to which people in the organization can refer when measuring their contribution. It is important in a learning organization that people within the organization have a collective understanding and vision of what the principles, goals, and purposes of the organization are. By making explicit the principles, goals, etc. of the organization, management transform a potentially alienated workforce into an integrated part of the whole (Senge, 1994).

When articulating the vision of the organization it is very important to incorporate the personal vision of how people see the organization into the overall vision of the organization as articulated by management (Guthrie, 1996). This type of institutional structure can be made part of the broader organization by emphasizing with a great degree of openness and clarity exactly what the vision of the organization is. To build a shared vision, individuals must be encouraged to hold and express their personal vision. These personal visions should form the basis for the formulation of a genuinely shared vision, which must itself be continually reviewed.

Team learning

Garvin (1993) advocates that not all learning comes from reflection and self-analysis. Indeed, some of the most powerful insights come from looking outside one's environment to gain new perspective and ideas. Team learning involves knowledge sharing and the utilization of knowledge in a collective thinking environment. Senge (1990) believes that teams, rather than individuals, are the basic learning units in modern organizations. The emphasis of team learning is on dialogue, which facilitates the examination of current assumptions that may inhibit learning. His philosophy behind incorporating these disciplines lies in the understanding that organizations are a product of how people think and interact; organizations cannot change in any fundamental way unless people change their basic processes of thinking and interacting.

O'Brien (1994) provided more 'tangible' building blocks that will enable organizations to achieve learning organization success. In their research, Bennett and O'Brien (1994) examined the practices that enabled 25 companies to apply the principles of organizational learning successfully, and arrived at twelve practices that will help build a learning organization. O'Brien (1994) stressed that no continuous learning practice is effective unless it is adopted as part of a system.

Personal mastery

Personal mastery is about the commitment individuals make with regard to their self-improvement. It encompasses continuous improvement in learning skills and competencies and engaging in continuous personal and professional development. A learning organization needs to support the development and application of this discipline among organization members. Personal mastery is an institutional and cultural idea that must occur within the organization at the individual level (from vice presidents down to researchers and workers) in the construction of the learning organization (Guthrie, 1996). For leadership within the learning organization, personal mastery means compassion, self and other acceptance, shared power, sensitivity, humility, tolerance, and the valuing of ambiguity (Garrat, 1994). Personal mastery is about gaining personal power and exercising control. According to Epictetus 'No man is free who is not a master of himself.'

Systems thinking

Systems thinking represents the cornerstone of a learning organization. Senge (1990) believed that individuals in a firm need to understand that business is a system and learn to look at its interrelated whole instead of focusing on snapshots. To develop systems thinking, individuals can take part in activities going on in different parts of the same organization. Systems thinking provides us with the ability to see the bigger picture by looking at the interrelationships of a system as opposed to simple cause–effect chains, allowing continuous processes to be studied rather than single pictures.

Senge (1990) sees systems thinking at the heart of his learning organization model, where all organization members develop an understanding of the whole rather than just fractional parts of the organization in terms of structures, processes, thinking, and behavior. 'Systems thinking' is the discipline that integrates the other disciplines, fusing them into a coherent body of theory and practice. It keeps them from being separate gimmicks or the latest fad for organizational change. Without a systemic orientation, there is no motivation to look at how the disciplines interrelate. By enhancing each of the other disciplines, it continually reminds us that the whole can exceed the sum of its parts.

Barriers and challenges

The learning organization as a concept is very interesting and appealing. Garvin (2000) noted that acceptance of the learning organization model has been high but progress toward achieving it has been slow. Much of the work done in this area is conceptual and practical steps toward achieving the status of learning organization must overcome many of the barriers to change. While many researchers seem to adopt the Senge model, which prescribes how to create a particular learning organization or describes those already formed as blueprints for managers to follow, this gives a false impression that achieving learning organization status is easy, which is far from the truth.

Knowledge sharing in general tends to be a difficult issue for organizations to tackle. As knowledge is personal, getting people to share without a system of reward and recognition in place is very difficult. Learning in the organization occurs when people are willing to share. But in many cases where people in the organization advance their own goals and objectives over those of the organization, then a type of selfish learning tends to take place. Pedler et al. (1991) highlighted that while learning could take place at the group/team level, selfish learning tended to occur when members use their learning for their own ends rather than for the benefit of the whole organization. This phenomenon can further lead to a situation where the interests and goals of the units concerned are seen as being more important than the overall goals of the whole organization. Organizations need to be conscious about selfish learning and implement a system of recognition and reward to align people's goals and objectives with those of the organization.

For many organizations, learning is not something high on the agenda and in many cases they try to push it aside as long as it is not considered critical to their projects or operations. Most commercial organizations are still very much concerned about the bottom line and need reassurance of the return on investment in implementing the learning organization. The lack of objective measures on the value and effectiveness of learning hinder the implementation of the learning organization. There are very few studies that attempt to show how the learning organization concept works to achieve performance improvement (Jacobs, 1995; Kaiser and Holton, 1998). Smith and Tosey (1999) acknowledged that evidence is even harder to come by of organizations linking learning to the return on investment and to the kinds of results that might convince businesses to spend money on a learning organization journey. Without such an assessment approach, they contend that even a preliminary exploration of the means to substantiate a business case for a learning organization is precluded.

It is important to align people's expectations with the organization's business objectives. If people feel that the organization is exploiting them and not paying much attention to their welfare and professional development, they will resort to selfish learning and try to advance their own business objectives rather than those of the organization. Megan (1996) pointed out that the energy and drive for learning should come from wanting to be the best in the business and that learning initiatives should be tied to core goals and competencies. Organizations that launch initiatives with the sole goal of becoming a 'learning organization' are likely to be disappointed with the results. If learning initiatives are adopted simply for the sake of learning, employees may become cynical and management credibility undermined. The learning organization is a journey that requires long-term practices that will involve everyone in the organization.

Finger and Brand (1999) argue that Senge's model favors individual and collective learning processes at all levels of the organization, but does not connect them properly to the organization's strategic objectives. It is imperative that the link between individual and collective learning and the organization's strategic objectives is made. Individual learning that is not in the organization's interests or in line with the organization's direction might result in a 'brain drain.' It is important to create an awareness within the organization of the importance of participating in the collective learning process. There is also a need for some form of measurement of organizational learning that enables the organization to assess the extent to which such learning contributes or not towards the strategic objectives.

Organizational culture plays an important role in shaping up the future of any learning organization. Argyris (1992) stated that the existence of defensive routines arising from a culture of blame and the resulting absence of learning from mistakes is a sure guarantee that the same problems tend to recur over time. Marsick and Watkins (1999) added that the culture in most organizations instills a fear of making mistakes, sending a mixed message about their tolerance of error which states that 'it is OK to experiment, but it is definitely not OK to fail.' While no one deliberately sets out to make mistakes, it is unlikely that breaking new ground will always be one hundred per cent successful.

Organizational culture is reflected in the corporate structure, leadership, and management style, and in the organization's attributes, norms, and practices. A multi-layered or flat hierarchy reflects the formality of an organization, which in turn affects the flow of information and hence of knowledge sharing and collaboration. Teare and Dealtry (1998) expressed their concern over culture that is traditionally hierarchical and competitive. Who is going to commit themselves to action learning, building a shared vision and team learning if they see their colleagues engaging in old-culture politics and succeeding, possibly, at the learners' expense?

Learning in an organization can take many forms. Learning can take place at the individual level or at the organization level. In both cases, learning initiatives often require sweeping changes throughout the organization. In many situations where change takes place quickly and without sufficient justification to convince staff, there is a danger that people will resist change and not see the importance of their participation. Failure to communicate the rationale and need for change might result in marginalizing the learning initiatives, pushing them into small pockets in the organization to end right there. Learning efforts must permeate the entire enterprise in order to be effective and long lasting. Senge et al. (1999) stated that the traditional model of change in which the change is led from the top has a less than impressive track record. He added that he had never seen a successful organizational learning programme rolled out from the top.

The lack of effective leadership can be seen as one of the barriers to the successful creation of generative learning organizations. Senge (1990) argues that learning organizations require a new view of leadership as opposed to the traditional view of leaders. Only a few people in the organization are usually able to set directions and make key decisions. The learning organization requires a fundamental rethinking of leadership. There must be a change in the old beliefs that only managers can make decisions and employees don't have to think on the job (Honold, 1991). Leadership in the learning organization requires the ability to coach and teach. It is not exclusive, authoritative or assumed, but learned and earned.

9

Knowledge management education

Introduction

There is a great deal of debate going on right now about the future of information professionals on the one hand and knowledge management as a profession on the other. The changing role of the information professional from gatekeeper to content manager and context specialist, and the move toward the knowledge economy by many industrialized nations, are clear indications of the transition. Many educational institutions around the world today are starting new knowledge management programs responding to market demands and trying to meet the aspirations of many of the information and knowledge professionals who would like to see themselves as knowledge leaders, knowledge managers and content specialists.

In the information and knowledge society, knowledge professionals are expected to assume higher responsibilities in dealing with the influx of information and oversee the management of organizational information resources and intellectual capital. They are expected to manage the process and ensure that business needs are served, develop high-level knowledge management strategies, and establish a knowledge management infrastructure.

As knowledge becomes a key strategic resource, there is a need to have a broader understanding of the various knowledge management processes that include knowledge creation, knowledge capture, knowledge retention, knowledge transfer, and knowledge sharing. We also need to have a better understanding of the process of identifying and leveraging existing knowledge resources. Universities and educational institutions (suppliers of knowledge) as well as private businesses and public sector organizations (users of knowledge) are in need of an integrative discipline for studying and learning about knowledge and its role in the economy. Identifying the skills and competencies of knowledge professionals can provide the basis for defining the requirements for the knowledge management profession. This will also help in determining the core modules needed for any knowledge management training program.

When knowledge management as a concept became popular in the late 1990s, many of the information technology vendors and management consultants jumped on the bandwagon and projected themselves as experts on the subject. This has led to many people questioning the notion behind knowledge management and wondering whether it is just another management fad. The lack of knowledge management qualifications has made it difficult to establish knowledge management work as a profession. At the heart of any profession is a set of qualifications and accepted entry requirements. Professional bodies such as computer societies, library associations, and engineering, legal, and medical bodies play an important role in defining their professions through certification and accreditation programs. Normally such programs support and enhance the professional education programs offered by university and educational institutions.

Many of the postgraduate programs in knowledge management launched by various universities around the world are closely associated with information studies and information systems programs. This is natural as information literacy and information technologies are very important components of knowledge management. While knowledge management is not about technology, technology is an important enabler of knowledge management as discussed in Chapter 4. Information literacy covers a wide range of skills and competencies that library and information science normally cater for. For knowledge management professionals such skills and competencies are needed to deal with the management of explicit knowledge or information. Knowledge professionals are also required to assist users in the organization in locating, filtering, and synthesizing much of the internal and external information.

The other reason for library and information studies schools to start knowledge management programs is the belief that failure to respond to this challenge will see other academic disciplines such as business or engineering schools moving to exploit the growing market for information and knowledge practitioners. In order to survive and thrive in an increasingly competitive educational marketplace, it is necessary to re-examine the approach to information studies education and take into account the changes in technology and the shift toward the knowledge economy (Milner, 1998). There is a need to equip information and knowledge professionals

Knowledge management presents the information profession with a unique opportunity to make an impact in organizations of all sizes and in all sectors. To take advantage of this opportunity, individual professionals need to fully understand the potential of those skills and the business objectives of the organizations that employ them. More fundamentally, we need a profession that represents the range of skills that is required to manage complex corporate information. However, it must be noted that knowledge management education is not exclusive to any particular sector. It must be open to all those who have the confidence and the skills to take advantage of the opportunities that exist. It is not surprising to find that in some instances, business schools are beginning to lay claim to areas of expertise that have traditionally been the mainstay of information departments. What is crucial is that they do so without any reference to professional bodies, or apparent sense of need for accreditation.

KM as an emerging profession

Knowledge management practices like knowledge-sharing activities, communities of practice, the learning organization, organizational learning, best practices, collaboration, and knowledge discovery are becoming popular and are starting to take root in many organizations. This is despite the fact that until now knowledge management has not been an established profession but rather is emerging and will continue to develop in the future. While most organizations today realize the value of knowledge and the need to improve knowledge management practices in their operations, there is very little consensus on who should be in charge or what types of profile knowledge management professionals should have.

Current knowledge management practitioners range from corporate strategists taking a knowledge approach, specialists in IT-based strategic developments, and marketing/corporate strategy professionals pursuing culture change initiatives for competitive advantage, to consultants using knowledge management as a method and human resource professionals leading management and organizational development programs in which knowledge creation, capture, sharing, and use play a main part.

Many organizations are still in the process of defining the knowledge management role, which in some involves a realignment or extension of existing roles. These roles have a variety of job titles with varying definitions, some explicitly labelled as knowledge management while others are information and IT-related. Titles such as chief knowledge officer (CKO), chief information officer (CIO), chief technology officer (CTO), knowledge developer, content manager, and knowledge executive are becoming popular as organizations start to create new positions and labels for those staff involved in their knowledge management initiatives. Table 9.1 shows a sample of possible knowledge management job titles. Professional organizations can also play an important role in this area by defining the types of competencies knowledge management professionals should acquire and the labels that should be attached to them.

It is important to note that many people believe that, by definition, knowledge management should not be concentrated in an individual or team of individuals, but instead every member of the organization should be involved in managing knowledge. It can in fact be argued that every employee of the organization should be involved in knowledge management practices. In an organization where knowledge management is not yet fully integrated into the working patterns of the entire workforce, there is a need for knowledge management champions who will enable knowledge management within the many diverse parts of the organization.

Although there is no need to have knowledge management departments similar to the IT or computer centers set up for information technology, there is still a need for knowledge professionals who see their roles as more like facilitators and communicators. They are people who can see the full picture and facilitate the knowledge activities within the organization. Knowledge professionals should be distinguished from knowledge workers in terms or role and competencies. While a knowledge worker is anyone in the organization who deals with knowledge-intensive work, the knowledge professional is someone who can act as a bridge between the knowledge workers and decision-makers. He or she has the skills necessary and competencies that enable them to deal with organizational knowledge and promote knowledge management practices within the organization.

Knowledge management as a profession is still emerging. New knowledge management roles and structures are appearing that

Table 9.1	Knowledge management related job titles
Knowledge-related job titles	Chief knowledge officer (CKO)
	Knowledge engineer
	Knowledge editor
	Knowledge analyst
	Knowledge navigator
	Knowledge architect
	Knowledge broker
	Knowledge asset manager
	Innovation officer/manager
	Knowledge integrator
	Knowledge leader
	Internal communications manager
Information-related job titles	Chief information officer (CIO)
	Information analyst
	Information architect
	Information innovator
	Content director
	Synthesizer
	Information developer
	Content analyst
	Librarian
	Documentation/configuration management
	Records manager
	Content manager
	Information officer/archivist
	Web content specialist
IT-related job titles	Chief technology officer (CTO)
	Senior IT architect
	System architect
	Network analyst
	Data manager
	Web designer
	Web developer
	System designer
	System developer
	System analyst
	Database manager
	Programmer
	Network administrator
	Technology manager
	Software analyst

are different from one organization to another. What knowledge management researchers and practitioners are hoping to achieve is to identify a set of common features and a rich mix of skills and competencies common to most organizations. The importance of a professional qualification in knowledge management is that, like any other profession, it helps to establish agreed upon and accepted entry requirements. The lack of a professional qualification in knowledge management will only serve to reinforce the misconception that anyone with common sense and a bit of exposure to the jargon can perform knowledge management work. The discussion and debate about knowledge management education and knowledge management as a profession will continue until consensus on the making of the discipline and the profession has been reached. There is a need for people who are involved in knowledge management education from different disciplinary backgrounds such as business schools, computer schools, library science schools, and social science and communication schools to come together and share their experiences and views on the emerging discipline.

Information and knowledge domains

It is clear that there are significant overlaps in the theories relating to the information and knowledge domains. It is important to understand these overlaps and distinguish the differences that will help in developing new and relevant knowledge management courses, rather than just re-naming the existing information management programs. To understand knowledge management and differentiate it from information management, let us look at the investment value diagram – or what I refer to as the utilization pyramid – shown in Figure 9.1. The investment value diagram differentiates between information management and knowledge management in terms of knowledge as a process and knowledge

Figure 9.1 Utilization pyramid

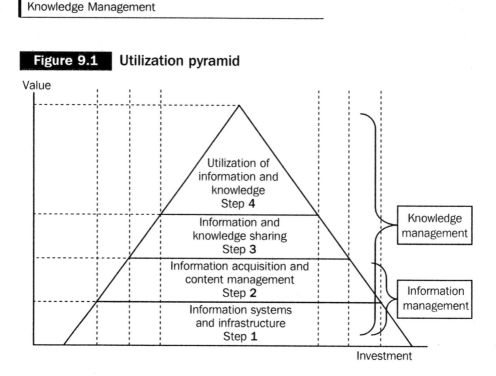

Value

Utilization of
information and
knowledge
Step 4

Information and
knowledge sharing
Step 3

Information acquisition and
content management
Step 2

Information systems
and infrastructure
Step 1

Knowledge
management

Information
management

Investment

as an object. It shows how organizations normally invest in information and knowledge management activities and the value these organizations normally get out of the investment. From the return on investment point of view, Figure 9.1 demonstrates clearly the return on investment in both information management and knowledge management combined. At the bottom of the utilization pyramid is the amount of investment an organization makes in information systems, networking, hardware, and software. Clearly, the return on investment in this category is not very high. Moving up the ladder, organizations also invest substantially in information acquisition, cataloguing, classification, taxonomies, and information retrieval. Content management is an important area and becoming problematic as the amount of information generated every day increases at incredible speed. Despite that, the return on investment in this area is not very high. While investment in steps 1 and 2 is very important to the organization and sometimes cannot be avoided, it is dangerous for an organization to assume that this is all they need to do and there is no need to go further.

Step 3 in the utilization pyramid shows the investment organizations make in information and knowledge-sharing activities and the value that can be derived from these activities. Clearly, the returns on investment are much higher in this category than the previous ones. It is a similar position with information use and utilization shown in step 4. Obviously what most organizations need to do is to pay more attention to information and knowledge-sharing activities and ensure that information and knowledge captured is utilized and translated into new products and services. While information management activities can be viewed as steps 1 and 2 in the utilization pyramid, knowledge management can be viewed as steps 1 to 4 in the utilization pyramid. This shows that information management is very important and forms a foundation to knowledge management. Knowledge management includes additional activities such as knowledge sharing and knowledge utilization beside those included in information management. Organizations need to increase investment in those areas that were not part of information management in the past but which also ensure higher returns and value to the organization.

From the utilization pyramid shown in Figure 9.1 we can also try to differentiate between the role played by information professionals in the past and the role that knowledge professionals need to play in the future. To a large extent we can argue that the role of information and IT professionals until recently was limited to steps 1 and 2 in the utilization pyramid. This is not to say that information professionals did not contribute to information and knowledge-sharing activities in the past, but that such a role was minimal and the emphasis was largely on information acquisition, organization and retrieval.

One can also argue that the lack of focus on knowledge management activities in the past is not really an information professional's problem but rather a failure on the part of the organization to realize the importance of information and knowledge-sharing activities. Information and knowledge utilization is a key to the development of new products and services in any organization. By realizing the importance of information and knowledge in the new economy, organizations start to embark on knowledge management initiatives to enhance their productivity and maintain competitiveness. In doing so, organizations will require, firstly, knowledge management performance measurements to help them assess the effectiveness of their knowledge management initiatives, and, secondly, knowledge management professionals or champions who will guide the knowledge management implementations within the organizations.

Unlike information professionals who, one might say, always associated themselves with the management of information as a profession, knowledge professionals could be anyone from any discipline and any profession, be it a doctor, engineer, lawyer, teacher, researcher or scientist, who understands the importance of knowledge and the value in sharing and utilizing both individual and organizational knowledge. What most organizations are trying to achieve from embarking on knowledge management initiatives is to increase their returns on investment, whether in monetary form or in the form of enhanced products and services. Organizations also need to increase investment and put more effort into ensuring that the information and knowledge that resides in databases, patents, trade secrets or the minds of people are utilized and translated into products and services that give value to the organization. If information and IT professionals are mainly concerned with steps 1 and 2 in the utilization pyramid, knowledge professionals are people who will be concerned with steps 1, 2, 3 and 4.

Given the high value that can be derived from knowledge management activities, organizations hope to make these practices part of their daily operations. They hope to recruit new breeds of knowledge professionals who can help them maximize the return on their investment. Using knowledge management technologies such as knowledge discovery tools, collaboration tools, and mind-mapping tools, organizations hope to enhance the information and knowledge utilization process. As knowledge management activities include information management, knowledge professionals need to acquire skills traditionally acquired by information and IT professionals. While information and IT professional competencies mainly focused on those included in steps 1 and 2 of the utilization pyramid, the skills of knowledge professionals need to be expanded to include steps 3 and 4. This means that knowledge professionals have to acquire skills and competencies needed by the four different steps in the utilization pyramid.

Associating disciplines with the four steps in the utilization pyramid helps in identifying the types of courses needed in knowledge management training. Information technology can be associated with step 1 in the pyramid. This involves hardware and software, system design, system development, network deployment, and infrastructure applications such as databases, data warehousing, intranets, portals, etc. Information and library science can be associated with step 2. This involves information acquisition, information organization, content management, metadata, taxonomies, ontology, classification, etc. Communication and cognitive science can be associated with step 3 in the pyramid. This focuses on human interactions, informal networks, human–computer interaction, communities of practice, organizational learning, cultural aspects, etc. Business and management can be associated with step 4 in the pyramid. This involves business strategies, the development of new products and services, improvements to existing products and services, marketing strategies, decision-making, innovation, intellectual property, etc.

It is clear that the knowledge management domain encapsulates the information management domain. As knowledge management is a multidisciplinary subject, Figure 9.2 give us an idea of the types of subjects and disciplines needed for knowledge management education. Knowledge management professionals need to have a strong background in information management. They will need to acquire IT and information science skills as a foundation, making it desirable to have people trained in IT and information studies to move into knowledge managment. The other competencies and skills needed are those related to tacit knowledge transfer. These require good communication skills as well as a good understanding of human behavior and cognitive science. Business and management skills are needed to enable knowledge professionals help create value and wealth for the organization.

Figure 9.2 **Discipline association**

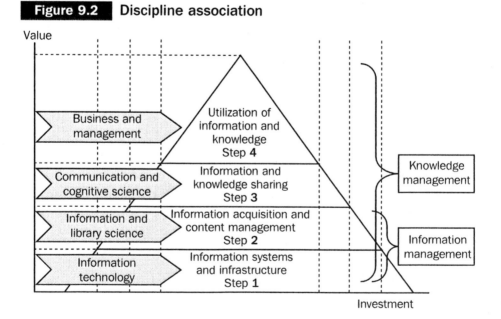

KM as a multidisciplinary profession

It is clear from Figure 9.2 that knowledge management is a multi-disciplinary profession. Knowledge professionals need to have a broader education that enables them to deal with a complex technological environment and the large amount of information generated every day, to encourage and promote knowledge-sharing activities, and to help in ensuring that information and knowledge acquired by the organization is utilized and translated into products and services.

One of the early attempts to look at knowledge management as a cross-disciplinary profession is that by Sveiby (1996) who viewed knowledge management as having an IT-track and a people-track. The IT-track focuses on the management of information. Proponents of this view tend to be researchers and practitioners educated in computer and information science. The knowledge management activities comprise the construction of information management systems, artificial intelligence, data mining, and other enabling technologies. To them, knowledge can be treated as objects that can be identified and handled by an information system. This perspective is fueled by the rapid developments in IT. For those who adopt the people-centred knowledge management perspective, knowledge management is about the management of people. Here, researchers and practitioners tend to be educated in philosophy, psychology, sociology, business, and management. The core knowledge management activities encompass assessing, changing, and improving individual human skills and behavior. These two perspectives do not converge on a very tidy view of the essence of knowledge management but clearly illustrate the importance of management science (especially human resources management and organizational theory) and information technology to knowledge managment.

According to Davenport and Cronin (2000), the interdisciplinary nature of knowledge management can be examined from the perspectives of three groups of professionals of distinctly different educational background. The three domains are library and information science, process engineering and organization theory. Library and information science deals with many aspects of knowledge management such as information acquisition, organization and retrieval, and reference and enquiry services, while process engineering has a strong systems orientation. The emphasis in process engineering is on the discovery and extraction of value when existing processes and resources are atomized and recompiled. In knowledge management, each individual becomes responsible for managing the knowledge that enables the successful implementation of the processes. The people in the third domain represent a growing recognition among analysts that the key to knowledge management is the interplay of tacit and explicit knowledge, and the primary task of managers is the conversion of 'human capital' into 'structural capital' (Stewart, 1997). Nonaka and Takeuchi's (1995) conceptual 'ba' – the space where 'knowing' happens – is a comprehensive expression of this perspective. It describes a continuous interplay in organizations of codified and uncodified, private and public knowledge that feeds the incremental conversion of tacit to explicit and explicit to tacit.

Looking to other disciplines in order to support knowledge management activities is an obvious and logical choice. According to Wiig (1999), disciplines in support of knowledge management include business theory and economics, cognitive sciences, cybrary sciences (library science and cyberspace), ergonomics to create effective and acceptable work environments, information sciences, knowledge engineering to elicit and codify knowledge, artificial intelligence to automate routine and assist knowledge-intensive work, management sciences to optimize operations and integrate knowledge management efforts with other enterprise efforts, and social sciences. This highlights the multidisciplinary nature of knowledge management and the need for a better understanding of the issues involved in managing all types of knowledge, including information. It is clear that information management is an important component of knowledge management and an understanding of information management principles is crucial. This would include some of the traditional core skills of library and information science such as indexing, classification, information retrieval, taxonomies, and so on.

Technology is a key enabler of knowledge management. However, knowledge management is much more than technology, but 'techknowledgy' is clearly a part of knowledge management (Davenport and Prusak, 2000). Information technology is emerging as an integrator of communications technology rather than solely as a keeper of information. The critical role of IT lies in its ability to support communication, collaboration, customer relations management, connecting communities of practice, and providing access to large depositories of information. Knowledge management technologies are developing rapidly due to an increase in demand by top global organizations, attention by consultants and integrators, and efforts by pioneering vendors (Natarajan and Shekhar, 2000). Hence, it is imperative that knowledge professionals understand existing knowledge management technologies and continue to follow and monitor the development of new and emerging technologies.

Communication and an understanding of human cognitive functions are also at the heart of knowledge management practices. It is important to incorporate better professional understanding of cognitive aspects of how knowledge–understanding mental models and their associations affect decision-making and the performance of knowledge-intensive work. Communication skills such as verbal, written, and presentation skills are important and required in order to influence, persuade, negotiate, and share knowledge (TFPL Ltd, 1999). Teams and communities feature high in knowledge management practices with team skills and community understanding becoming increasingly important. Building multi-disciplinary teams in order to achieve knowledge management objectives requires people and management skills. This is because a knowledge management agenda can only be forwarded through influence, persuasion, and demonstration. It is critical that knowledge professionals possess good communication skills and are able to interact with the knowledge workers in the organization.

Some of the benefits organizations can gain from knowledge management practices include innovation, efficiency, improved decision-making, increased responsiveness to customers, flexibility, quality improvement, a reduction in duplication, and empowerment. Many of these issues are business and management issues. Management science examines the different methods used in decision-making and solving managerial problems, and also develops interpersonal skills for working in interdisciplinary teams. Management science education serves to provide a broad-based knowledge of managing as a process and function in organizations as well as to develop problem-solving and analytic skills. Knowledge professionals need to understand the business model of the organization (Chen, Chiu, and Fan, 2001).

Figure 9.3 shows the four different disciplines needed as a minimum to support knowledge management activities. The four disciplines are information technology, information and library science, communication and cognitive science, and business and management. The ability to derive a set of core modules from these disciplines is key to the establishment of knowledge management as a career. Crafting any knowledge management curriculum will depend largely on the set of skills and competencies knowledge professionals have to acquire to be able to do the job. Some of these skills and competencies will be discussed in the next section.

Figure 9.3 KM as a multidisciplinary topic

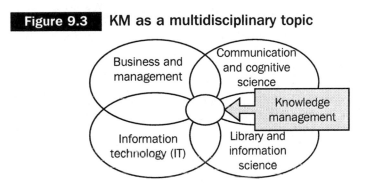

Roles and competencies of knowledge professionals

As more and more organizations adopt the use of knowledge management methods and practices, the need for trained and qualified knowledge management professionals will continue to grow. The uncertainty and confusion over the necessity for knowledge management roles is mirrored in the roles themselves. This can be seen in the variety of titles that can be found for knowledge management professionals, both at managerial levels and below. At managerial level, for example, Skandia has a director of intellectual capital, Buckman Laboratories has a global director of intellectual assets, and Dow Chemical has a global director of intellectual capital (Davenport and Prusak, 2000).

Debra Amidon, founder of Entovation International, listed eight categories of knowledge jobs that included knowledge management professionals within the category (*http://www.entovation.com*):

1. Knowledge and innovation professionals who shape and formulate knowledge-based programs.

2. Knowledge management professionals who have expertise in knowledge management implementation.

3. Knowledge cataloguers, researchers, and media specialists who have skills in Web technology, the Internet, libraries, and content development.

4. Knowledge and competitive intelligence professionals who are able to create and develop positions and have online research savvy and good presentation skills.

5. Knowledge and strategic integration professionals, such as thinkers, planners, and marketers.

6. Knowledge academicians, theorists, and visionaries who focus primarily on discussion within an academic setting as well as developing and testing models and applications.

7. Knowledge facilitators, trainers, and corporate educators who focus on learning and education in a corporate setting.

8. Knowledge and expert systems professionals whose primary focus is information technology.

In another research project funded by the UK Library and Information Commission to gain an understanding of the knowledge management roles, skills, and competencies needed in these environments, a similar set of profiles to categorize knowledge management practitioners was identified. The roles identified include knowledge leaders, knowledge managers, knowledge navigators, knowledge synthesizers, content editors, webmasters, and knowledge brokers, as well as those involved in coaching and mentoring roles (Abell and Oxbrow, 1999). A simpler definition is to divide knowledge management roles into those leading knowledge management initiatives and those implementing them. In line with this, Reynolds (2000) proposes that knowledge sharing is best supported by a two-part organizational structure with professional, dedicated knowledge management staff who own the knowledge processes, templates, and technologies, and knowledge sponsors, integrators, and developers from the business units who own the knowledge content.

The formulation of a consistent job specification for knowledge professionals remains an elusive task. Different organizations are likely to have different expectations and as a result create different jobs with different titles and different labels for the various knowledge activities that are taking place. Job titles assigned to information professionals are likely to influence their role in the organization and affect their ability to implement the needed changes. The perception and credibility of the job have an impact on the status of the knowledge professional. It is important to note that many of the knowledge management roles that are evolving today as a result of knowledge management activities have become career development roles for many of those interested in knowledge management. Common features of these roles are a good grasp of the subject matter, an ability to relate to organizational needs, flexibility and willingness to take on tasks outside their own professional area, and the ability to be persuasive. People who are able to take advantage of an opportunity and convince others that they are up to the task have developed their skills and competencies through interaction with the rest of the knowledge management community. These skills can be either perceived or articulated based on current practices in other areas such as information technology, library and information science or business and management.

In a study that examined the role of information professionals in the context of managing knowledge within an organization, Al-Hawamdeh and Ritter (2000) carried out a survey of 73 participants from the private sector and government agencies in Singapore. They found that the information professionals' roles need redefinition to deal with both formal and informal knowledge within the organization. Information professionals in this context refer to anyone who is responsible for the transfer of information and knowledge in the organization. They may hold diverse titles such as project manager, database manager, customer relations manager, information specialist, documentation specialist, information manager, knowledge manager, and so on. They apply their knowledge to create value for the organization and are responsible for managing the creation, capture, synthesis, sharing, and application of the collective intelligence of the organization. They will manage the process to ensure that business needs are served, develop high-level knowledge management strategies, and create a knowledge management infrastructure. Turning information into solutions, information professionals piece information together and reflect on their experience, generate insight, and use this insight to solve problems (McDermott, 1999).

A skill and competencies set based on the findings was identified from the study (see Figure 9.4). This included the need for information professionals to have a good overall understanding of the business and organization, and creativity in gathering information and creating synergy from the use of information. They also need to proactively anticipate and respond to changes in the environment, be lifelong learners, exhibit self-learning capabilities, and demonstrate self-control and problem-solving skills. Finally they must promote a culture of sharing information and knowledge, and be knowledgeable and competent in adapting applications of new technologies in their organization.

Figure 9.4 **Skills needed by information specialists (n = 73)**

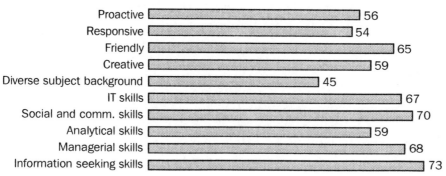

Figure 9.5 shows an alternative presentation of these competencies and skill sets for information and knowledge specialists in the information economy (Foo and Al-Hawamdeh, 2001). This has been grouped into the six categories of skills: IT skills, information skills, communication skills, leadership and management skills, analytical skills, and personal characteristics. These competencies can serve as a useful basis for curriculum design for educating and transforming information professionals in the new workplace.

These competencies and skills are similar in many ways to those proposed for a chief knowledge officer in a public sector organization by Neilson (2001) that includes the six main categories: tools and technology skills, communications, leadership and management, personal knowledge and cognitive capability, strategic thinking, and personal behavior. competence in these skills allows the knowledge professional to fulfill a number of roles in the organization, including: providing leadership and strategy, measuring outcomes, promoting 'best' practices and processes, creating a knowledge-sharing culture, championing communities of practice, using incentives and rewards, creating and using a taxonomy (common language), securing resources, providing tools and technology, and championing education in the organization.

This, in some ways, indicates that information professionals are already educated and trained to exhibit a number of such important skills. With the addition of an appropriate mix of the missing skills set, they are poised to take on the expanded role of knowledge work and play a key role in the emerging information and knowledge-intensive organization.

Figure 9.5 Competencies and skills set of knowledge professionals

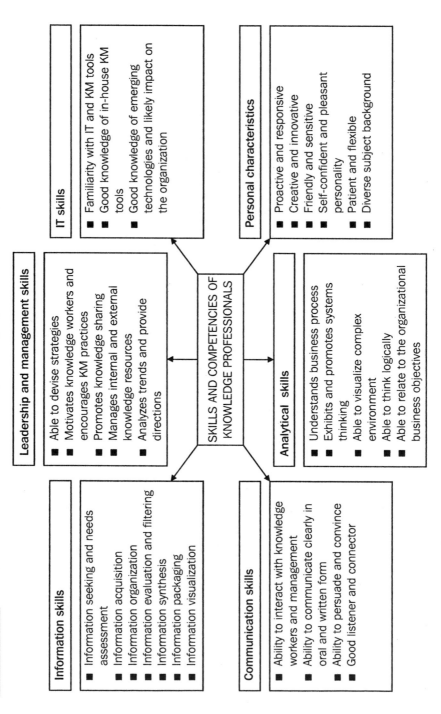

Information skills

- Information seeking and needs assessment
- Information acquisition
- Information organization
- Information evaluation and filtering
- Information synthesis
- Information packaging
- Information visualization

Leadership and management skills

- Able to devise strategies
- Motivates knowledge workers and encourages KM practices
- Promotes knowledge sharing
- Manages internal and external knowledge resources
- Analyzes trends and provide directions

IT skills

- Familiarity with IT and KM tools
- Good knowledge of in-house KM tools
- Good knowledge of emerging technologies and likely impact on the organization

SKILLS AND COMPETENCIES OF KNOWLEDGE PROFESSIONALS

Communication skills

- Ability to interact with knowledge workers and management
- Ability to communicate clearly in oral and written form
- Ability to persuade and convince
- Good listener and connector

Analytical skills

- Understands business process
- Exhibits and promotes systems thinking
- Able to visualize complex environment
- Able to think logically
- Able to relate to the organizational business objectives

Personal characteristics

- Proactive and responsive
- Creative and innovative
- Friendly and sensitive
- Self-confident and pleasant personality
- Patient and flexible
- Diverse subject background

Graduate programs in knowledge management

Normally it takes a while for industry practices to find their way into academia. Knowledge management is no exception. In the last ten years, there has been an influx of information about the subject, be it in the form of publications, books, magazines, or conference proceedings. Yet, as of today, there is only a small number of universities around the world that offer graduate programs in knowledge management. A graduate program will most likely be close in concept and impact to that of the Master of Business Administration (MBA). The MBA has always been viewed as the key qualification for the ambitious manager, and in recent years there has been an increase in the number of MBA programs and the specialization offered under that umbrella. While an MBA on its own might not guarantee recruitment for many managers, it provides an added value to their existing qualifications and enables them to gain an in-depth knowledge of a particular aspect of business. A graduate degree in knowledge management can also been seen as an added-value degree that enables managers and knowledge management practitioners to gain in-depth knowledge in various aspects of knowledge management that enhances their current position.

Beside the fact that knowledge management is business oriented and context dependent, information technology and information science are essential components in managing knowledge. A program in business and management alone would not satisfy the requirements and the competencies identified earlier in this chapter. Koenig (1999) argued that knowledge management is clearly information and knowledge driven, and programs in library and information science are therefore relevant. At the same time, a study by TFPL Ltd (1999) showed that people employing library and information science skills in a knowledge environment do not necessarily come from the information profession. Many of the traditional library and information studies skills are invaluable but need to be applied in a new context and linked to business processes and core operations. Communications and social skills are very important in tacit knowledge transfer. Any knowledge management program needs to emphasize the importance of communication skills and integrate certain aspects of communication and cognitive science into the curriculum.

Knowledge management is multidisciplinary and interdisciplinary. Being multidisciplinary makes it difficult to identify the make-up and nature of the disciplines involved. The difficulty in defining these disciplines resembles to a large extent the inability to arrive at an acceptable definition of knowledge management. The differences in opinion might be at the philosophical level and the views vary between those who view knowledge as object (knowledge is information) and those who view knowledge as process (knowledge is tacit and cultural), and learning as individual cognitive development or social construction. By the same token, knowledge management being interdisciplinary in nature can draw upon the theories and practices of existing disciplines.

The current knowledge management graduate programs offered by higher education institutions around the world do reflect the fact that knowledge management curriculums are inter-disciplinary. However, the choice of subjects taught in any knowledge management education program is not necessarily based on any objective assessment of what managers might need to know. It is much more likely to be based on the skills and knowledge available within the administering schools. Nonetheless, while it is true that, depending on the core discipline, the administering school tends to propose a syllabus that has more subjects in that discipline (e.g. an information science school offering knowledge management will have a library and information science biased track while a computer science school offering knowledge management will stress the IT aspects), what is evident is that the respective curricula of all the knowledge management programs evaluated show an interdisciplinary scope. In terms of administering schools or faculties, the active promoters for knowledge management education were observed to be from either library and information science or business schools.

Knowledge management education will continue to evolve and draw upon support from many theoretical and methodological areas. The education of knowledge management will continue to rely on new approaches that integrate theoretical and abstract perspectives of epistemology and cognitive science with the pragmatic considerations of expertise required to conduct business, and have the practical technical expertise found in information management and technology. The appendix lists some of the current graduate programs in knowledge management. It contains information about the schools offering the programs, admission criteria and core modules offered by the programs.

Appendix

Graduate programs in knowledge management

School/university	Copenhagen Business School
Course/program	Master of Knowledge Management
URL	*http://www.masterkm.net*
Admission requirements	The MKM program only accepts applicants who as a minimum hold a bachelor's degree (or equivalent). In addition, applicants should be able to document at least three years of professional (post-university), full-time employment. Management experience as well as international experience is highly appreciated. Fluency in English is required. Some applicants will be asked to perform an IELTS language test.
Sample modules	■ Classics in Management and Organization ■ Buzzing around KM ■ KM Technologies ■ Knowledge Leadership ■ Business and Knowledge Strategy ■ Innovation Project ■ Knowledge Sharing and Networking ■ Master Thesis

School/university	Cranfield University
Course/program	MSc (Knowledge Management Systems)
URL	*http://barrington.rmcs.cranfield.ac.uk/prospectus/postgrad/*
Admission requirements	Normally a second-class honors degree or equivalent; however, in exceptional cases a candidate may be admitted with appropriate professional experience. Students not having English as their native tongue must also attain an IELTS score of 7.
Sample modules	■ Foundations of Knowledge ■ Organizational Knowledge ■ Knowledge Management ■ Knowledge Management Systems ■ Knowledge Representation ■ Knowledge Programming ■ Knowledge Storage and Sharing ■ Knowledge Discovery ■ Knowledge Interfaces ■ Knowledge Engineering ■ Project Dissertation and Oral Examination

School/university	Dominican University
Course/program	MSc (Knowledge Management)
URL	*http://www.dom.edu/gslis/ckm.html*
Admission requirements	A baccalaureate degree from an institution accredited by a nationally recognized regional accrediting association; official transcripts from all schools attended; undergraduate GPA of 3.0 or better on a 4.0 scale; satisfactory scores on the Graduate Management Admission Test (GMAT), the Graduate Record Examination (GRE) or the Miller Analogies Test (MAT).
Sample modules	■ Knowledge Management ■ Organizational Analysis and Design ■ Management Information Systems ■ Knowledge Technologies

- Information Policy
- Organization of Knowledge
- Capstone Course/Practicum
- Competitive Intelligence for Management Decision making

School/university	Donau University, Austria
Course/program	Master of Advanced Studies (KM)
URL	*http://www.donau-uni.ac.at/en/weiterbildung/lg_ basis38.html*
Admission requirements	Academic degree and/or a minimum of four years relevant professional experience; knowledge of German and English.
List of courses	Not available.

School/university	George Mason University
Course/program	Masters of Science in New Professional Studies (with concentration in Knowledge Management)
URL	*http://psol.gmu.edu/*
Admission requirements	To be considered for admission to degree status applicants must have at least a bachelor's degree from an accredited institution, *an approved certificate from the National Defense University*, and relevant work experience, and must meet the general admission requirements for graduate study. Admission is based on a departmental admissions committee's evaluation of the applicant's suitability.
Sample modules	■ The New Professionalism: Theory and Practice (Understanding Knowledge and the Knowledge Organization)
	■ The New Professional as Reflective Practitioner (Managing the Knowledge Organization)
	■ Technology and Learning in the New Professions (Using Technology to Support Knowledge Sharing)
	■ Research Methodologies in the New Professionalism (Working with Communities in Knowledge Organizations)

- International Strategic Management
- International Issues in Knowledge Management
- E-Commerce and the Digital Divide
- Economics of Electronic Commerce
- Critical Information Technology Infrastructures

School/university	**George Washington University**
Course/program	Masters of Engineering Management with concentration in KM MSc with concentration in KM
URL	*http://gwu.edu/km/programs.cfm*
Admission requirements	*For Masters of Engineering Management or Masters of Science with concentration in KM* Students applying for degree candidacy must meet the entrance requirements of the School of Engineering and Applied Science (SEAS). A bachelor's degree with a minimum 2.5 grade point average (on a 4.0 scale or the equivalent) from an accredited university is generally required.
Sample modules	■ Knowledge Management I ■ KM: Leadership and Management ■ The Learning Enterprise ■ Knowledgeware Technologies ■ KM: Organization and Processes ■ Knowledge Management II

School/university	**Kent State University**
Course/program	MSc (Information Architecture and Knowledge Management)
URL	*http://iakm.kent.edu/kmcurric.html*
Admission requirements	An undergraduate degree with a minimum 3.0 (A = 4) grade point average; satisfactory scores on the Graduate Record Examination/TOEFL and/or appropriate professional experience; evidence of computer literacy.

Sample modules	■ Information Architecture and Knowledge Management I
	■ Information Architecture and Knowledge Management II
	■ Information Design in the Digital Age
	■ Structure of Computer Science
	■ Information Technologies
	■ Strategic Information Management
	■ Economics of Information
	■ Research Methods in Communication
	■ Quantitative Methods in Business Administration I
	■ Research Methods in Mass Communication
	■ Research for Decision Making in Libraries and Information Centers
	■ Master's Project

School/university	Lancaster University
Course/program	MA (Human Resource and Knowledge Management)
URL	*http://www.lums.lancs.ac.uk/pages/Postgraduate/ MAHRMandKM*
Admission requirements	First- or second-class honors degree (or equivalent high level GPA) in psychology, sociology or one of the related social sciences or a first- or second-class honors degree (or equivalent high level GPA) in another discipline backed by significant administrative, managerial or industrial experience.
Sample modules	■ Organizational Analysis I: The Politics of Contemporary Organizational Change
	■ Organizational Analysis II: Structural Transitions
	■ The Management of Organizational Change
	■ Knowledge Management and Information Technology
	■ Human Resource Management I
	■ Human Resource Management II: Advanced HRM
	■ Science and Theory in Management and Organization Studies

- Research in Organizational Settings
- Dissertation

School/university	**Loughborough University**
Course/program	MSc (Information and Knowledge Management)
URL	*http://www.lboro.ac.uk/prospectus/pg/taught/sci/ infoknow.htm*
Admission requirements	Good degree in any discipline
Sample modules	

- Design and Authoring for the World Wide Web
- Information Retrieval for Knowledge Management
- Informatics and KM Systems
- Principles of Knowledge Management
- Information Architecture
- Competitive Intelligence
- Legal and Professional Issues
- Management of Innovation and Entrepreneurship
- Management Techniques and People Skills
- Information and Knowledge Management in the NHS

School/university	**Monash University**
Course/program	Masters of Information Management and Systems with specialization in KM
URL	*http://www.sims.monash.edu.au/courses/ pgrad/mims/specialisations/km.html*
Admission requirements	Applicants for admission must normally have qualified for a bachelor's degree at a satisfactory level at Monash University or at another tertiary institution approved by the Faculty of Information Technology. Special entry provisions enable admission to candidates without formal tertiary qualifications who have extensive relevant professional experience.

Sample modules	■ Knowledge Management (compulsory)
	■ OLAP and Business Intelligence
	■ Reading unit (special topics in Knowledge Management)
	■ Information Enterprise Management and Marketing
	■ Electronic Document Management and Recordkeeping Systems
	■ The Information Continuum

School/university	Multimedia University
Course/program	Masters in Knowledge Management with Multimedia
URL	*http://www.mmu.edu.my/knowledge_management/toughtmaster_page/taught_main.htm*
Admission requirements	A minimum second-class honors bachelor's degree from the Multimedia University or any other recognized university; or candidates with a degree from Multimedia University or any other recognized university with at least two years' relevant working experience.
Sample modules	■ History and Concepts of Knowledge Management
	■ Knowledge Management Application
	■ Human Communication and Knowledge Management
	■ Multimedia and Information Technology
	■ Strategic Knowledge Management I
	■ e-Knowledge Management
	■ Interactive Multimedia Development
	■ Organizational Learning
	■ Dissertation

School/university	**Nanyang Technological University**
Course/program	MSc (Knowledge Management)
URL	*http://www.ntu.edu.sg/sci/is/km.htm*
Admission requirements	Candidates should have a first degree in any discipline with at least three years' working experience.
Sample modules	■ Information and Knowledge Society
	■ Information and Knowledge Sources
	■ Foundations of Knowledge Management
	■ Knowledge Management Tools
	■ Communication and Organizational Behaviour
	■ Internet Technologies and Applications
	■ Business Intelligence
	■ Electronic Records and Document Management
	■ Electronic Commerce and Knowledge Management
	■ Technopreneurship and Venture Creation
	■ Knowledge Management Measurement
	■ Knowledge Management in the Public Sector

School/university	**Nottingham University, Business School**
Course/program	MSc (Enterprise Knowledge Management)
URL	*http://www.nottingham.ac.uk/business/ma/ N1DT13.htm*
Admission requirements	Candidates for the MSc Programme should normally have, or expect to gain, a first- or good second-class honors degree in a related subject, such as management, business studies, marketing, economics, accounting and finance.
Sample modules	Not available

School/university	**Robert Gordon University, School of Information and Media**
Course/program	MSc (Knowledge Management)
URL	*http://www.rgu.ac.uk/prospectus/disp _ProspSearch.cfm*

Admission requirements	Not available
Sample modules	■ Knowledge Management: Philosophy and Roles ■ Information Studies ■ Knowledge Management: Tools and Technology ■ The Business Context of Human Resource Management ■ Knowledge Management Systems ■ Technology and Culture ■ Research Methods ■ Fieldwork Placement ■ Dissertation

School/university	**Royal Roads University**
Course/program	MBA in Executive Management with specialization in KM MA (KM)
URL	*http://www.royalroads.ca*
Admission requirements	*For MBA in Executive Management with Specialization in KM* Work experience is a key requirement of admission to the program. It is expected that most of the applicants will have already earned an undergraduate degree. However, this may not be an absolute requirement in all cases. *For MA (KM)* Relevant work experience is a key requirement of admission to the program. As a guideline, at least five years' experience working with issues related to knowledge management. Candidates should also have an undergraduate degree or the equivalent combination of post-secondary education and professional accredited qualifications.
Sample modules	*For MBA in Executive Management with specialization in KM* ■ Leadership Development Workshops ■ Environment of Business

- Creative Leadership
- Organizational Relations
- Marketing Management
- Financial and Managerial Accounting
- Research Methods
- Intellectual Capital and Intellectual Property
- Knowledge Management Foundations and Processes
- Organization and Management Information Systems

For MA (KM)

- Strategies and Foundations of Knowledge Management
- Culture and Leadership for Building Knowledge Capital
- Technologies for Knowledge Management
- Organization and Management Information Systems
- Standards and Knowledge Management
- Intellectual Capital and Intellectual Property
- Advanced Techniques in the KM Environment
- Knowledge Management and Sustainability
- Catalyzing Change (Research Methods for Knowledge Management)
- Communities of Practice

School/university	**Singapore Institute of Management**
Course/program	Master of Knowledge Management (MA (KM) awarded by University of Melbourne)
URL	*http://www1.sim.edu.sg/sim/pub/gen/sim_pub _gen_content.cfm?mnuid=152&ID=146*
Admission requirements	A three-year degree in an appropriate discipline. Appropriate disciplines may include: information technology/computer science, engineering, management/business administration, education, economics, organizational psychology and records management; and at least two years of documented

relevant work and/or professional experience. Applicants may be required to undertake an IELTS or TOEFL test as proof of competency in English, if their first degree is from an institution in which the language of instruction is not in English (required score: IELTS – 7, TOEFL – 600).

Sample modules
- Principles of Knowledge Management
- Business Fundamentals for Knowledge Managers
- Applying Knowledge Management
- Information Systems Impact and Change Management
- Creating and Utilizing New Knowledge
- Creating Knowledge Cultures
- Information Systems in an International Context
- Developing Knowledge in the Systematic Enterprise
- Contextualizing Knowledge Management
- Work-based Project

School/university	**South Bank University**
Course/program	MSc (Knowledge Management Systems)
URL	*http://www.cios.sbu.ac.uk/kms/About_KM.html*
Admission requirements	Not available
Sample modules	

- Knowledge Management Technology
- Perspectives of and on Knowledge Management
- Computational Intelligence for Knowledge Management
- Knowledge Management Strategies
- Knowledge Management Practice
- Research Methods for Knowledge Management
- Selecting and Acquiring Knowledge Management Systems
- Evaluating Knowledge Capital and Assets
- Dissertation (Knowledge Management Systems)

School/university	University of Canberra
Course/program	Masters of Knowledge Management
URL	*http://www.ce.canberra.edu.au/flexmasters/ km.htm*
Admission requirements	A four-year undergraduate degree; or an honors degree; or a three-year undergraduate degree and at least two years' relevant work experience; or a graduate diploma; or academic qualifications deemed to be equivalent by the University's Admissions Committee; or various combinations of study or learning gained from work experience.
Sample modules	■ Knowledge Management Principles
	■ Knowledge Management Processes
	■ Knowledge Management Systems
	■ Knowledge Management Leadership
	■ Knowledge Management
	■ Issues in Online Management
	■ Information Analysis and Retrieval

School/university	University of Central England
Course/program	MSc (Knowledge Management)
	MSc (Knowledge Organization and Management)
URL	*http://www.uce.ac.uk/web2/business/km.html*
Admission requirements	*For MSc (Knowledge Management)* A post-graduate Diploma in Management Studies or its equivalent.
	For MSc (Knowledge Organization and Management) To apply for the course, students should have successfully completed an honors degree and have some appropriate experience in information work and a recognized Information and Library Studies qualification. Individuals with other qualifications and experience will be considered and applications are welcomed from those who believe they could benefit from the courses.
Sample modules	Not available.

School/university	University of Central England in Birmingham, Business School
Course/program	MSc (Knowledge Management)
URL	*http://www.tbs.uce.ac.uk/default.asp?pageID=89*
Admission requirements	A postgraduate diploma in management or equivalent professional qualifications in HR, marketing or finance; PgDip Public Administration etc. with a core syllabus in management theory and practice at strategic level.
Sample modules	■ Knowledge Strategy ■ Knowledge Systems ■ Action Research on Knowledge Management in Organizations

School/university	University of Central England in Birmingham, Faculty of Computing Information and English
Course/program	MSc (Knowledge Organization and Management)
URL	*http://www.cie.uce.ac.uk/SIS/Pgrad/msc_kn_org_man.htm*
Admission requirements	To apply for the course students should have successfully completed an honours degree and have some appropriate experience in information work and a recognized Information and Library Studies qualification. However, the faculty will be happy to consider individuals with other qualifications and experience.
Sample modules	■ Introduction to Knowledge Management ■ Information and Knowledge Audit ■ Records Management ■ Organizational Change and Development ■ Specialist Study ■ Project Management

School/university	University of Melbourne
Course/program	Masters of Knowledge Management Postgraduate Diploma in Knowledge Management Postgraduate Certificate in Knowledge Management

URL	*http://www.edfac.unimelb.edu.au/EPM/COLL/ KMcourse/UnimelbPgradKM.pdf*
Admission requirements	Completed a three-year degree in an appropriate discipline (such as education, economics, organizational psychology, records management) with at least two years of documental relevant work and/or professional experience.
Sample modules	■ Principles of Knowledge Management ■ Business Fundamentals for Knowledge Managers ■ Strategy ■ Technologies for Managing Information ■ Knowledge Management and Organizational Learning

School/university	**University of North London, Computing and Information Management**
Course/program	MSc (Information and Knowledge Management)
URL	*http://www.unl.ac.uk/postgradline/ikm.html*
Admission requirements	Not available
Sample modules	■ Managing Information in the Organization ■ Managing Knowledge ■ Information and Knowledge Resources: Organization and Management ■ Legal Perspectives on IKM ■ Research and Evaluation Strategies for IKM ■ Information and Knowledge Management Project ■ Knowledge Applications

School/university	**University of Oklahoma, School of Library and Information Studies**
Course/program	MSc (Knowledge Management)
URL	*http://www.ou.edu/cas/slis/degreeprogs/ mskm.htm*
Admission requirements	An applicant may be granted full graduate standing if: all required documentation has been

submitted and determined to be complete; *and* the applicant has been determined to be acceptable for admission to the Graduate College; *and* the applicant's academic record indicates a grade point average of at least 3.20 for the last 60 hours of letter-graded undergraduate course work *or* has completed a master's degree or at least 12 semester hours of letter-graded graduate course work with a cumulative 3.00 grade point average for all graduate work; *and* the applicant submits valid Graduate Record Examination scores.

Sample modules
- Foundations of Information Studies
- Organization of Information
- Design and Implementation of Networked Information Services
- Knowledge Representation
- Knowledge Management Design Project
- The Psychology of Leadership
- Managing Creativity
- Seminar in Leadership in Organizations
- Seminar in Organizational Change and Development
- Creative Problem Solving

School/university	**University of South Australia**
Course/program	MA (Knowledge Management)
URL	*http://www.unisa.edu.au/*
Admission requirements	Students will normally have a recognized undergraduate degree from an Australian university or equivalent. Students who have completed the Graduate Diploma in Knowledge Management will be eligible for entry into the Master of Arts (Knowledge Management).
Sample modules	■ Information Pathways

- Strategic Information Management
- Theories and Concepts in Knowledge Management
- Knowledge Representation

- The Learning Organization
- Organization Structure, Culture and the Knowledge Worker
- Information, Systems and Competitive Advantage
- Information Economics
- Competitive Intelligence
- Information Discourse Ethics
- Organization of Knowledge
- Thesis: Knowledge Management Part A
- Thesis: Knowledge Management Part B
- Issues in Knowledge Management
- Applied Graduate Project in Knowledge Management

School/university	University of Technology Sydney
Course/program	Graduate Diploma (Knowledge Management)
URL	*http://datasearch.iim.uts.edu.au/courses/ allcourses/results.lasso*
Admission requirements	To gain entry to this course an applicant must demonstrate a strong level of education, background, and capability. It is expected that applicants will have an undergraduate degree or equivalent and that they will have demonstrated a high level of interest in, and some knowledge of, information and knowledge practices.
Sample modules	- Enabling Information Access
	- People, Information and Knowledge
	- Knowledge and the Organization
	- Information Seminars
	- Knowledge Management Strategies
	- Knowledge Management Systems
	- Information Initiative
	- Electronic Information Systems Design
	- Business Information and Intelligence
	- Virtual Information Collections, Resources and Services

Bibliography

Abell, A. and Oxbrow, N. (1999) 'Skills for the knowledge economy: the reality of the market place,' *Business Information Review*, 16(3), 115–21.

Adalian, P.T. Jr, Hoffman, I.M., Rockman, I.F. and Swanson, J. (1997) 'Internet-based experiential learning in international marketing: the case of Globalview.org,' *Reference Service Review*, 25(3), 11–22. Retrieved from Emerald database.

Al-Hawamdeh, S. (2002) *Communication and Cultural Resistance: Formulating a Knowledge Management Strategy in a Public Sector Organization.* Proceedings of the Australian Conference on Knowledge Management and Intelligent Decision Support (AKMIDS), Melbourne, Australia.

Al-Hawamdeh, S. and Hart, T.L. (2002) *Information and Knowledge Society.* Singapore: McGraw-Hill Education.

Al-Hawamdeh, S. and Ritter, W. (2000) 'Managing formal and informal knowledge within organisation: re-defining the role of information professionals,' in *Proceedings of 2000 The Knowledge Management Conference* (KMAC 2000), Birmingham, UK, pp. 277–83.

American Productivity and Quality Center (APQC) (2001) *Socializing Knowledge Management.* Retrieved 15 December 2001, from *http://www.apqc.org/free/articles/dispArticle.cfm?ProductID=1348.*

Amrit, T. (2000) *The Knowledge Management Toolkit: Practical Techniques for Building a Knowledge Management System.* Englewood Cliffs, NJ: Prentice-Hall.

Ang, S. and Joseph, D. (1996) 'Organizational learning and learning organizations: triggering events, structures and processes,' in *Academy of Management Meeting*, 9–14 August 1996, Cincinnati, Ohio.

Anton, J. (1996) *Customer Relationship Management: Making Hard Decisions with Soft Numbers.* Upper Saddle River, NJ: Prentice-Hall.

Argyris, C. (1992) *On Organizational Learning.* Oxford: Blackwell Business.

Argyris, C. and Schon, D.A. (1996) *Organizational Learning II: Theory, Method and Practice.* Reading, MA: Addison Wesley.

Ash, J. (2000) 'Building a knowledge sharing culture,' *Knowledgepoint Intellectual Capital* article. Retrieved 12 September 2001 from *http://www.knowledgepoint.com.au/intellectual_capital/Articles/IC_JA001.htm.*

Barclay, R.O. and Murray, P.C. (1997) *What Is Knowledge Management?* Retrieved 11 November 2001 from *http://www.media-access.com/whatis.html.*

Barth, S. (2000) 'Miles to go,' *Knowledge Management Magazine*, *http://www.destinationkm.com/articles/default.asp?ArticleID=868.*

Beckman, T. (1999) 'The current state of knowledge management,' in *Knowledge Management Handbook.* Boston: CRC Press.

Bennett, J.K. and O'Brien, M.J. (1994) 'The building blocks of the learning organization,' *Training*, 31(6), 41–51.

Bessant, J. and Pavitt, K. (1997) *Managing Innovation: Integrating Technological, Market and Organisational Changes.* Chichester: Wiley.

Bobrow, D. (1999) *Eureka: Sharing Best Practices in Field Service*. San José, CA: Benchmarking Institute.

Bonaventura, M. (1997) 'The benefits of a knowledge culture,' *Aslib Proceedings*, 49, 82–9.

Bontis, N. (1996) 'There's a price on your head: managing intellectual capital strategically,' *Business Quarterly*, Summer, 40–7.

Bontis, N. (2001) 'Assessing knowledge assets: a review of the models used to measure intellectual capital,' *International Journal of Management Review*, 3(1), 41–60.

Bontis, N. and Dragonetti, C.N. (1999) 'The knowledge toolbox: a review of the tools available to measure and manage intangible resources,' *Journal of European Management*, 17(4), 391–402.

Brabston, M.E. and McNamara, G. (1998) 'The Internet as a competitive knowledge tool for top managers,' *Industrial Management and Data Systems*, 98(4), 158–64.

Brailsford, T.W. (2001) 'Building a knowledge community at Hallmark Cards,' *Research Technology Management*, September/October.

Brooking, A. (1996) *Intellectual Capital: Core Assets for the Third Millennium Enterprise*. London: Thomson Business Press.

Brown, J.S. and Duguid, P. (in press) 'Enacting design,' in P. Adler (ed.), *Designing Automation for Usability*. New York: Oxford University Press.

Chen, H.H., Chiu, T.H. and Fan, J.W. (2001) 'Educating knowledge management professionals in the era of knowledge economy,' *Proceedings of the International Conference on Library and Information Science Education (ICLISE)*, Kuala Lumpur, Malaysia.

Chew, L.L. and Al-Hawamdeh, S. (2001) 'Government initiatives and the knowledge economy: case of Singapore,' in *Proceeding of the Conference on Human.Society@Internet. Lecture Notes in Computer Science*. Seoul, South Korea: Springer-Verlag, pp. 19–32.

Cohen, D. and Prusak, L. (2001) *In Good Company: How Social Capital Makes Organizations Work*. Boston, MA: Harvard Business School Press.

Conner, D.R. (1998) *Leading at the Edge of Chaos: How to Create the Nimble Organization*. New York: John Wiley & Sons.

Cordeiro, M.C. and Al-Hawamdeh, S. (2001) 'National Information Infrastructure and the realization of Singapore IT2000 Initiative,' *Information Research Journal*, 6(2). Retrieved from *http://informationr.net/ir/6-2/paper96.html*.

CSIS International Communications Studies Program (1994) *Japan and the United States: Revving Up for the Information Superhighway*, including highlights of the Japan–US Information Infrastructure Symposium, 13 June 1994, International Conference Hall of the United Nations University, Tokyo, Japan. Washington, DC: CSIS International Communications Studies Program.

Davenport, E. and Cronin, B. (2000) *Knowledge Management: Semantic Drift or Conceptual Shift?* Retrieved from *http://www.alise.org/conferences/conf00_Davenport-Cronin_paper.htm*.

Davenport, T. and Prusak, L. (1998) *Working Knowledge: How Organizations Manage What They Know*. Cambridge, MA: Harvard University Press.

De Long, D.W. and Fahey, L. (2000) 'Diagnosing cultural barriers to knowledge management,' *Academy of Management Executive*, 14(4), 113–27.

De Long, D., Davenport, T. and Beers, M. (1997) *What Is a Knowledge Management Project?* Retrieved 1 September 2001 from *http://www.cbi.cgey.com/cgi-bin/pubs.plx?sort=authorv.*

Deal, T. and Kennedy, A.A. (1982) *Corporate Cultures.* Reading, MA: Addison-Wesley.

Denning, S. (2001) *The Springboard: How Storytelling Ignites Action in Knowledge-Era Organizations.* Boston: Butterworth-Heineman.

Dibella, A.J. and Nevis, E.C. (1997) *How Organizations Learn: An Integrated Strategy for Building Learning Capability.* San Francisco: Jossey-Bass.

Drucker, P.F. (1994) 'The age of social transformation,' *Atlantic Monthly,* 274(5), 53–80.

Duffy, J. (1999) *Harvesting Experience – Reaping the Benefits of Knowledge.* Prairie Village, KS: ARMA International.

Duffy, J. (2001) 'The tools and technologies needed for knowledge management,' *Information Management Journal,* 35(1), 64–7.

Earl, M. (2001) 'Knowledge management strategies: toward a taxonomy,' *Journal of Management Information Systems,* 18(1), 215–33. Retrieved 24 November 2001 from Academic Search Premier database.

Edvinsson, L. and Malone, M.S. (1997). *Intellectual Capital: Realizing Your Company's True Value by Finding Its Hidden Brainpower.* New York: Harper Business.

Edwards, A.D.N. (1995) 'The rise of the graphical user interface,' *Information Technology and Disabilities,* 2(4). Retrieved 30 November 2001 from *http://www.rit.edu/~easi/itd/itdv02n4/article3.html.*

Edwards, C. (2001) 'Global knowledge: a challenge for librarians,' in the *66th IFLA Council and General Conference,* Jerusalem, Israel, 13–18 August 2001. Retrieved from *http://www.ifla.org/IV/ifla66/papers7153–154e.htm.*

Federal Interagency Forum on Aging-Related Statistics (FIFARS) (2000) *Older Americans 2000: Key Indicators of Well-Being.* New York: FIFARS.

Finger, M. and Brand, S.B. (1999) 'The concept of the "learning organization" applied to the transformation of the public sector,' in M. Easterby-Smith, L. Araujo and J. Burgoyne (eds), *Organizational Learning and the Learning Organization.* London: Sage.

Foo, S. and Al-Hawamdeh, S. (2001) 'Educating knowledge professionals through a graduate program in information studies: a Singapore perspective,' in *Proceedings of the 3rd Digital Library Conference: Positioning the Fountain of Knowledge.* Sarawak, Malaysia: Kuching, Pustake Negri Sarawak.

Foray, D. and Lundvall, B.D. (1996) 'The knowledge-based economy: from the economics of knowledge to the learning economy,' in *Employment and Growth in the Knowledge-Based Economy.* Paris: OECD, pp. 11–32.

Franklin, S. and Mary, P. (2001) 'Managing change: the use of mixed delivery modes to increase learning opportunities,' *Australian Journal of Educational Technology,* 17(1), 37–49. Retrieved 7 August 2001 from *http://cleo.murdoch.edu.au/ajet/ajet17/franklin.html.*

Galpin, T. (1996) *The Human Side of Change: A Practical Guide to Organization Redesign.* San Francisco: Jossey-Bass.

Garrat, B. (1994) *The Learning Organization.* London: HarperCollins.

Garvin, D. (1997) 'How to build a learning organization,' condensed from presentation to *The International Conference on Strategic Manufacturing.* Retrieved 28 August 2001 from *http://www.european-quality.co.uk/articles/garvin.html.*

Garvin, D. (2000a) 'Learning organizations at work: Harvard B-school Professor David Garvin discusses learning in action,' *New Corporate University Review*. Retrieved 23 August 2001 from *http://www.traininguniversity.com/magazine/july_aug00/cover1.html*.

Garvin, D.A. (2000b) *Learning in Action – A Guide to Putting the Learning Organisation to Work*. Boston, MA: Harvard Business School Press.

GIIC Asia Regional Meeting and International Conference (1995) 'National Information Infrastructure for Social and Economic Development in Asia,' in C.A. Charles (ed.), *GIIC Asia Regional Meeting and International Conference*, 28–30 November 1995, Bangkok, Thailand. Organized by the Global Information Infrastructure Commission (GIIC), National Electronics and Computer Technology Center, Thailand.

Gongla, P. and Rizzuto, C.R. (2001) 'Evolving communities of practice: IBM global services experience,' *IBM Systems Journal*, 40(4): 842–62.

Gould, D. (1997) *Leading Virtual Teams*. Retrieved 14 January 2002 from *http://www.seanet.com/~daveg/ltv.htm*.

Gratton, M. (1993) 'Leadership in the learning organization,' *New Directions for Community Colleges*, 21(4), 93–103.

Guthrie, D. (1996) *Transforming an Existing Organization into a Learning Organization*. Retrieved 28 August 2001 from *http://www.gdss.com/wp/transform.htm*.

Hadley, K. (1997) 'Creating buy in for your strategic plan,' *Ideas for Your Success*. Available at *http://www.fed.org/onlinemag/aug97/hadley.html*. Accessed 25 August 2003.

Hamel, G. and Prahalad, C.K. (1994) *Competing for the Future*. Boston: Harvard Business School Press.

Henson, M.T. (1999) 'The search-transfer problem: the role of weak ties in sharing knowledge across organization subunits,' *Administrative Science Quarterly*, 44, 82–111.

Honold, L. (1991) 'The power of learning at Johnsonville Foods,' *Training*, 28(4), 55–8.

Horngren, C.T., Foster, G. and Datar, S. (1997) *Cost Accounting: A Managerial Emphasis*. Englewood Cliffs, NJ: Prentice-Hall.

Housel, T. and Bell, A.H. (2001) *Measuring and Managing Knowledge*. Boston: McGraw-Hill Higher Education.

Huang, K.T. (1998) 'Capitalizing on intellectual assets,' in J.W. Cortada and J.A. Woods (eds), *The Knowledge Management Yearbook 1999–2000*. Oxford: Butterworth-Heinemann, pp. 346–66.

Inkpen, A.C. and Dinur, A. (1998) 'Knowledge management processes and international joint ventures,' *Organization Science*, 9, 454–68.

Jacobs, R. (1995) 'Impressions about the learning organization: looking to see what is behind the curtain,' *Human Resource Development Quarterly*, 6(2), 119–22.

Johnston, R. and Rolf, B. (1998) 'Knowledge moves to centre stage,' *Science Communication*, 20(1), 99–105.

Junnarkar, B. and Brown, C.V. (1997) 'Re-assessing the enabling role of information technology,' *Journal of Knowledge Management*, 1(2), 142–8.

Kaiser, S.M. and Holton, E.E. (1998) 'The learning organization as a performance improvement strategy,' in R. Torraco (ed.), *Proceedings of the Academy of Human Resource Development Conference*. Oak Brook, IL: Academy of Human Resource Development, pp. 75–82.

Kaplan, R.S. and Norton, D.P. (1992) 'The balanced scorecard measures that drive performance,' *Harvard Business Review*, January–February, 71–9.

Kaplan, R.S. and Norton, D.P. (1996) *The Balanced Scorecard: Translating Strategy into Action*. Boston: Harvard Business School Press.

Kappe, F. (2001) Hyperwave Information Server: Technical White Paper [Technisches White Paper]. Available at *http://www .hyperwave.com.*

Karlenzig, W. (1999) *Senge on Knowledge.* Retrieved 24 November 2001 from *http://www.destinationcrm.com/km/ dcrm_km_article.asp?id=55&ed=7%2F1%2F99.*

Kline, P. and Saunders, B. (1993) *Ten Steps to a Learning Organization.* Arlington, VA: Great Ocean Publishers.

Knowledge Management: Big Challenges, Big Rewards (1999). Retrieved 6 September 2002 from *http://www.cio.com/ sponsors/091599_km_1.html.*

Kochikar, V.P. (2000) *The Knowledge Maturity Model: A Staged Framework for Leveraging Knowledge.* Paper presented in the World Knowledge Forum, 13–15 September, Santa Clara Convention Center, Santa Clara, California.

Koenig, M. (1999) 'Education for knowledge management,' *Information Services and Use,* 19(1), 17–32.

Kotter, J. (1995) 'Leading change: why transformation efforts fail,' *Harvard Business Review,* March–April: 59–67 (reprint no. 95204).

Kotter, J. (1996) *Leading Change.* Boston, MA: Harvard Business School Press.

Kramer, R.M. and Tyler, T.R. (eds) (1996) *Trust in Organizations: Frontiers of Theory and Research.* Thousand Oaks, CA: Sage.

Kuan-Tsae, H. (1977) 'Capitalizing collective knowledge for winning, execution and teamwork,' *Journal of Knowledge Management,* 1(2), 149–57.

Lassey, P. (1998) *Developing a Learning Organization.* London: Kogan Page.

Lee, C.K. and Al-Hawamdeh, S. (2002) 'Factors impacting knowledge sharing,' *Journal of Information and Knowledge Management,* 1(1), 49–56.

Lee, S.M. and Hong, S. (2002) 'An enterprise-wide knowledge management system infrastructure,' *Industrial Management*, 102(1), 17–25.

Leonard-Barton, D. (1995) *Wellsprings of Knowledge: Building and Sustaining the Sources of Innovation*. Boston, MA: Harvard Business School Press.

Leow, B.G. (2000) *Census of Population 2000: Advance Data Release*. Singapore: Singapore Department of Statistics.

Lesser, E.L. and Storck, J. (2001) 'Communities of practice and organizational performance,' *IBM Systems Journal*, 40(4), 831–41.

Levitt, B. and March, J.G. (1988) 'Organization learning,' *Annual Review of Sociology*, 14, 319–40.

Levitt, T. (1989) 'Management and knowledge,' *Harvard Business Review*, 67(3), 8.

Liebowitz, J. (1998) 'Expert systems: an integral part of knowledge management,' *Kybernetes*, 27(2), 170–5.

Loh, M. (2001a) 'The human factor,' *Business Times: Knowledge Management Asia*, 17 July. Retrieved from *http://business-times-asia1-com-sg/supplement/story/0,2276,14755,00.html*.

Loh, M. (2001b) *The Human Factor*. Retrieved 21 August 2001 from *http://www.business-times.asia1.com.sg/supplement/story/0,2276,14755,00.html*

Luthy, D.H. (1998). *Intellectual Capital and Its Measurement*. Retrieved from *http://www3.bus.osaka-cu.ac.jp/apira98/archives/htmls/25.htm*.

Lytle, R.H. (1999) 'Asynchronous learning networks for knowledge workforce learning,' *Journal of Asynchronous Learning Networks*. Retrieved 24 November 2001 from *http://www.aln.org/alnweb/journal/vol3_issue1/JALN3_1_ma.htm*.

McAllister, D.J. (1995) 'Affect and cognition based trust as foundation for interpersonal cooperation in organizations,' *Academy of Management Journal*, 38(1), 24–59.

McDermott, R. (1999) 'Nurturing three dimensional communities of practice: how to get the most out of human networks,' *Knowledge Management Review*, Fall.

McDermott, R. (2000) 'Community development as a natural step,' *Knowledge Management Review*, 3(5): 16–19.

McDermott, R. and O'Dell, C. (2001) 'Overcoming barriers to sharing knowledge,' *Journal of Knowledge Management*, 5(1), 76–85.

McElroy, M.W. (1999) *Integrating Complexity Theory, Knowledge Management and Organizational Learning*. Retrieved 27 November 2001 from *http://www .macroinnovation.com/images/Integrating Complexity.pdf*.

McGill, J. and Beaty, L. (1992) *Action Learning – A Practitioner's Guide*. London: Kogan Page.

McGill, M.E., Slocum, J.S. and Lei, D. (1992) 'Management practices in learning organizations,' *Organizational Dynamics*, 21(1), 5–17.

Mack, R., Ravin, Y. and Bird, R.J. (2001) 'Knowledge portals and the emerging digital knowledge workplace' [electronic version], *IBM Systems Journal*, 40(4), 925–55.

Mah, A.Y. (1999) *Chinese Cinderella: The True Story of an Unwanted Daughter*. New York: Bantam Books.

Malhotra, Y. (1998) *Knowledge Management, Knowledge Organizations and Knowledge Workers: A View from the Front Lines*. Retrieved 15 March 2001 from h*ttp://www.brint.com/ interview/maeil.htm*.

Mann, F. and Neff, F. (1961) *Managing Major Change in Organizations*. Ann Arbor, MI: Foundation of Research on Human Behavior.

Marquardt, M.J. (1996) *Building the Learning Organisation*. New York: McGraw-Hill.

Marsick, V. and Watkins, K. (1999) 'Looking again at learning in the learning organization: a tool that can turn into a weapon,' *Learning Organization*, 6(5), 207–11.

Marwick, A.D. (2001) 'Knowledge management technology,' *IBM Systems Journal*, 40(4), 814–30.

Megan, S. (1996) *Reality Check*. Retrieved from *http://www.cio.com/archive/060196_uneasy_5.html*.

Mentzas, G. (2001) *An Holistic Approach to Realising the Full Value of Your 'Knowledge Assets'*. Retrieved 10 November 2001 from Academic Search Premier database.

Messmer, E. and Mears, J. (2002) 'Web portals pose security challenge.' Available at *http://www.nwfusion.com/news/2002/0114portals.html*. Accessed 25 August 2003.

Miller, D. and Slater, D. (2000) *The Internet: An Ethnographic Approach*. Oxford and New York: Berg.

Milner, E. (1998) 'The train is now leaving … the challenges of educating information professionals for the twenty-first century,' *Business Information Review*, 15(4), 243–7.

Mishra, A.K. (1996) 'Organizational responses to crisis: the centrality of trust,' in R. Kramer and T. Tyler (eds), *Trust in Organizations*. Thousand Oaks, CA: Sage, pp. 261–87.

Murray, P. (2000) 'Designing for business benefits from knowledge management,' in *Knowledge Horizons*. Boston: Butterworth-Heinemann.

Narayanan, V.K. (2001) *Managing Technology and Innovation for Competitive Advantage*. Englewood Cliffs, NJ: Prentice Hall.

Natarajan, G. and Shekhar, S. (2000) *Knowledge Management: Enabling Business Growth*. Boston, MA: McGraw-Hill.

Neef, D. (1999) *Little Knowledge Is a Dangerous Thing: Understanding Our Global Knowledge Economy.* Boston: Butterworth-Heinemann.

Neilson, R.E. (2001) *Knowledge Management and the Role of the Chief Knowledge Officer.* Information Resources Management College, National Defense University. Retrieved February 2001 from *http://www.ndu.edu/ndu/irmc/km-cio_role/km-cio-role.htm.*

Ng, A.K. (2001) *Why Asians Are Less Creative than Westerners.* Singapore: Prentice-Hall.

Nonaka, I. (1991) 'The knowledge-creating company,' *Harvard Business Review,* 71(6), 96–104.

Nonaka, I. and Takeuchi, H. (1995) *The Knowledge Creating Company: How Japanese Companies Create the Dynamics of Innovation.* New York: Oxford University Press.

O'Brien, M.J. (1994) *Learning Organization Practices Profile.* San Diego, CA: Pfeiffer.

O'Dell, C. and Grayson, C.J. Jr (1998) *If Only We Knew What We Know.* New York: Free Press.

Oliver, S. (1997) *Corporate Communication.* London: Kogan Page.

Palmer, J. (1998) 'Human organisation,' *Journal of Knowledge Management,* 1(4), 294–307.

Pedler, M., Burgoyne, J. and Boydell, T. (1991) *The Learning Company: A Strategy for Sustainable Development.* London: McGraw-Hill.

Polanyi, M. (1958) *Personal Knowledge: Towards a Post-Critical Philosophy.* Chicago: University of Chicago Press.

Polanyi, M. (1966) *The Tacit Dimension.* New York: Doubleday.

Price, D.J.d.S. (1961) *Science Since Babylon.* London: Yale University Press.

Price, D.J.d.S. (1963) *Little Science, Big Science.* New York: Columbia University Press.

Probst, G.J.B. and Buchel, B.S.T. (1997) *Organizational Learning.* Prentice Hall.

Probst, G., Raub, S. and Romhardt, K. (1999) *Managing Knowledge: Building Blocks for Success.* London: John Wiley & Sons.

Pulic, A. (2000) *An Accounting Tool for IC Management.* Retrieved from *http://www.measuring-ip.at/Papers/ham99txt.htm.*

Quinn, J., Baruch, J. and Zien, K. (1997) *Innovation Explosion: Using Intellect and Software to Revolutionise Growth Strategies.* New York: Free Press.

Quirke, B. (1995) *Communicating Change.* London: McGraw-Hill.

Reynolds, J. (2000) *Knowledge Management Club: Report on KM Skills Requirements.* CCTA Consultancy. Retrieved from *http://www.ogc.gov.uk/km/reports/skills_report.pdf.*

Roos, J., Roos, G., Dragonetti, N.C. and Edvinsson, L. (1997) *Intellectual Capital: Navigating in the New Business Landscape.* London: Macmillan.

Rosenberg, M.J. (2001). *Reinventing Training.* Retrieved 24 November 2001 from *http://www.destinationcrm.com/km/dcrb_km_article.asp?id=371.*

Schein, E. (1985) *Organizational Culture and Leadership.* San Francisco: Jossey-Bass.

Schein, E.H. (1993) 'On dialogue, culture, and organizational learning,' *Organizational Dynamics*, 22(2), 40–51.

Senge, P.M. (1990) *The Fifth Discipline: The Art and Practice of the Learning Organization.* London: Century.

Senge, P.M. (1994) *The Fifth Discipline Fieldbook: Strategies and Tools for Building a Learning Organization.* London: Nicholas Brealey.

Senge, P.M. et al. (1999) *The Dance of Change: The Challenges to Sustaining Momentum in Learning Organizations.* New York: Doubleday.

SingHealth (2001) *Siamese Twins Emerge Resilient After Marathon Separation Operation.* Retrieved 30 November 2001 from *http://www.singhealth.com.sg/News/news_load.asp?AnnounceID=20.*

Skyrme, D. (2000) *The Learning Organization.* Retrieved 24 November 2001 from *http://www.skyrme.com/insights/3lrnorg.htm.*

Slater, S.F. and Narver, J.C. (1995) 'Market orientation and the learning organization,' *Journal of Marketing*, 59, 63–74.

Smith, C. and Tosey, P. (1999) 'Assessing the learning organization: Part 1 – Theoretical foundations,' *Learning Organization*, 6(2), 70–5.

Smith, H.A. and McKeen, J.D. (2001) *Instilling a Knowledge Sharing Culture.* Retrieved 10 September from *http://www.alba.edu.gr/OKLC2002/Proceedings/pdf_files/ID25.pdf.*

Smythe, D. (1999) 'Facing the future: preparing new information professionals,' *Information Management Journal*, April, 44–8.

Snowden, D.J. (2000) 'Cynefin, a sense of time and place: an ecological approach to sense making and learning in formal and informal communities,' in *2nd Asia Pacific Conference on Knowledge Management.* Hong Kong Productivity Council.

Stamp, D. (2000) 'Communities of practice: learning is social. Training is irrelevant?' Available at *http://www.co-i-l.com/coil/knowledge-garden/cop/learnsoc.shtml.*

Stewart, G. (1995) 'EVA® works – but not if you make these common mistakes,' *Fortune*, 1 May, 117–18.

Stewart, T.A. (1990) 'The cunning plots of leadership,' *Fortune*, 138(5), 165–7.

Stewart, T.A. (1991) 'Brainpower,' *Fortune*, 123(11), 44–60.

Stewart, T.A. (1996) 'The invisible keys to Success,' *Fortune*, 6 August.

Stewart, T.A. (1997) *Intellectual Capital: The New Wealth of Organizations*. New York: Doubleday/Currency.

Storck, J. and Hill, P.A. (2000) 'Knowledge diffusion through "strategic communities,"' *Sloan Management Review*, Winter.

Sugarman, B. (1996) 'The learning organization and organizational learning: new roles for workers, managers, trainers and consultants,' Lesley College. Retrieved from *http://www.lesley.edu/faculty/sugarman/loandtd.htm*.

Szulanski, G. (1996) 'Exploring internal stickiness: impediments to the transfer for best practice within the firm,' *Strategic Management Journal*, 17 (Winter Special Issue), 27–43.

Sveiby, K.E. (1996) *What Is Knowledge Management?* Retrieved from *http://www.sveiby.com/articles/KnowledgeManagement.html*.

Teare, R. and Dealtry, R. (1998) 'Building and sustaining a learning organisation,' *Learning Organization*, 5(1), 47–60.

TFPL Ltd (1999) *Skills for Knowledge Management*. London: TFPL Ltd. Retrieved from *http://www.lic.gov.uk/ publications/executivesummaries/kmskills.html*.

Thomas, S. (1996) 'The invisible keys to success,' *Fortune*, 6 August.

Tissen, R., Andriessen, D. and Deprez, F.L. (1998) *Value-Based Knowledge Management: Creating the 21st Century Company: Knowledge Intensive, People Rich*. Amsterdam: Addison Wesley Longman.

Trotter, A. (2001) 'Cyberschool,' *Teacher Magazine*. Retrieved 7 August 2001 from *http://www.edweek.org/tm/tm_printstory.cfm?slug=08cyber.h12*.

Ullrich, R. and Wieland, G. (1980) *Organization Theory and Design*, revised edn. Homewood, IL: Richard D. Irwin.

UNESCO (n.d.) *World Information and Communication Report, 1999–2000*. UNESCO.

US Bureau of Labour (BLS) Releases 2000–2010 Employment Projections. (n.d.). Retrieved 3 December 2001 from *http://stats.bls.gov/news.release/ecopro.toc.htm*.

US Department of Commerce (2001) *Bureau of Economic Analysis: National Accounts Data*. GDP news release of 30 November 2001. Retrieved from *http://www.bea.doc.gov/bea/dn1.htm*.

Wakin, E. et al. (1999) *Into the Networked Age: How IBM and Other Firms Are Getting There Now*. New York: Oxford University Press.

Ward, A. (2000) 'Getting strategic value from constellations of communities,' *Strategy and Leadership*, March/April.

Watson, J.K. and Fenner, J. (2000) 'Understanding portals,' *Information Management Journal*, 34(3), 18–22.

Wee, C.H., Lee, K.S. and Bambang-Walujo, H. (1991) *Sun Tzu: War and Management*. Singapore: Addison-Wesley.

Wenger, E. (1998) 'Communities of practice: learning as a social system,' *Systems Thinker*, June.

Wenger, E., McDermott, R. and Snyder, W.M. (2002) *Cultivating Communities of Practice*. Boston: Harvard Business School Press.

Wiig, K.M. (1999) 'What future knowledge management users may expect,' *Journal of Knowledge Management*, 3(2), 155–65.

World Bank (2001) *Knowledge Sharing*. Accessed 25 August 2003 from *http://www.worldbank.org/ks/km_overview.html*.

World Trade Organization (1996) 'World trade expanded strongly in 1995 for the second consecutive year; robust trade growth expected this year,' 22 March, WTO News Press/44. Retrieved from *http://www.wto.org/english/news_e/pres96_e/pr044_e.htm*.

Yu, A. (1998) *Creating the Digital Future: The Secrets of Consistent Innovation at Intel.* New York: Free Press.

Zack, M.H. (1998) *Managing Codified Knowledge.* Retrieved 2 September 2001 from *http://www.cba.neu.edu/~mzack/articles/ kmarch/kmarch.htm.*

Zand, D. (1997) *The Leadership Triad: Knowledge, Trust, and Power.* Oxford: Oxford University Press.

Index

access control, 76
accreditation, 160
actors framework, 86
adaptive learning, 147
Africa, 6
apprenticeship, 125
archiving, 15
artificial intelligence, 169
ask the expert, 75
asymmetry, 111
audio conferencing, 79
authentication, 76
automated teller machines, 11

Balanced Scorecard, 39, 48, 49, 51, 52, 56
behavior, 102
best practice, 81, 91, 160
brainstorming, 130
Brazil, 6
bulletin boards, 77
business intelligence capital, 28, 38

calculated intangible value, 45, 46
calendaring, 61
capital and structural capital, 55
cartographic school, 29
cataloging, 164
categorization, 70, 74
channel, 88

chat sessions, 77
chief information officer, 160
chief knowledge officer, 160, 177
chief technology officer, 160
citation-weighted patents, 40, 42
classification, 75, 164, 167
climate, 90, 148
code of ethics, 116
codification, 18
cognitive science, 167, 170, 172
collaboration, 14, 77, 109, 160
    tools, 14, 64, 65, 92, 167
collaborative applications, 61
combination, 23, 24, 96
commercial school, 30
commitment, 116, 118
common interest, 122
communication, 31, 88, 92, 115, 118, 170
communication skills, 168
communities of practice, 51, 59, 79, 82, 121, 125, 126, 129, 130, 131, 132, 136, 160, 167
    evolution of, 131
    fostering, 133
community, 130
competencies, 9, 18, 19, 35, 79, 94, 95, 128, 139, 140, 158, 161, 163, 159, 177
competition, 27, 38

Printed in the United States
20407LVS00002B/23